PSALM TWENTY-FIVE &
PTSD

ROBERT SCHOLTEN

PSALM TWENTY-FIVE &
PTSD

A JOURNEY INTO THE DARKENED REALMS OF
POST TRAUMATIC STRESS DISORDER

TATE PUBLISHING & Enterprises

Published by Tate Publishing & Enterprises, LLC
127 E. Trade Center Terrace | Mustang, Oklahoma 73064 USA
1.888.361.9473 | www.tatepublishing.com

Tate Publishing is committed to excellence in the publishing industry. The company reflects the philosophy established by the founders, based on Psalm 68:11,
"The Lord gave the word and great was the company of those who published it."

Book design copyright © 2011 by Tate Publishing, LLC. All rights reserved.
Cover design by Kristen Verser
Interior design by Chelsea Womble

Published in the United States of America

ISBN: 978-1-61777-166-8
1. Religion, Christian Life, Personal Growth
2. Religion, Christian Life, Inspirational
11.03.01

Psalm 25 and PTSD is dedicated to all my fellow veterans of all wars.

Secondly, I dedicate this book to the loving memory of my mother, Grace, who loved me in spite of me and who prayed me through life until the day she closed her eyes only to have them opened in a far greater place.

Thirdly, I dedicate this book to my immediate and extended family who never gave up on me nor ever will because we are family. Our heritage has proven this blessing thus far.

ACKNOWLEDGMENTS

Proofreaders: I am terrible at spelling, and my computer spell-check agrees with me. Therefore, I am deeply grateful for the expertise of Silvia Hoksbergen, Jake Moss, Cheryl Scholten, and Yolanda Webb of Jackson County Ministries for their great spelling abilities and patience.

Family: My precious wife, Cheryl, and daughters, Lisa Joy and Hannah, are to be commended for their great love, patience, and understanding hearts toward me over the decades. They are a constant encouragement from which I draw strength to press on with my writing in spite of the effects of PTSD and a stroke in my life.

ARC and JCM: The Bible instructs us in Matthew 5:41 to "go the extra mile." Annville Community Reformed Church, for which I volunteer as pastor, and Jackson County Ministries, for which I voluteer as family life advisor, have both gone far beyond that mandate. Their compassion, love, and mercy enabled me the freedom to write *Psalm 25 and PTSD*.

Tate Publishing: I thank Tate Publishing for accepting *Psalm 25 and PTSD* for publication and distribution and for their encouragement during the transition of manuscript to book.

Prince of Peace: Words cannot express my gratitude to Jesus Christ, the Prince of Peace: who ushered me into the reality of salvation and security therein to the glory of God, the Father Almighty.

TABLE OF CONTENTS

FOREWORD

A Veteran's Perspective

In this book Robert has so eloquently written, I found chapters that really mirrored my experience with PTSD. The effort to hide it and man up is how most of us try to handle PTSD. Eventually it catches up with you, and it gets worse the older you get. Robert, who became a minister, handled his demons more inwardly than some of us, like me. I showed anger and emotional outbreaks and was confrontational, while other veterans used drugs and alcohol.

This book pulls the reader into the very pitfalls of combat veterans. I, like Robert, had to rely on my upbringing to bring God into the trench with me. Robert's book showed me that the things he suffered were some of the very things I suffered, and I thought I was the only one who had those afflictions. It helped me realize I am not the only one who has these thoughts and responses.

Robert's relationship with the Almighty is far more exceptional than most of ours, and the fact he suffers also tells us we are not alone. God's help is there if only we reach for that help. As we all know, we never recover from

PTSD, but maybe we can put it in perspective and deal with it. I highly recommend this book as a must-read for veterans with PTSD.

In fact, anyone desiring to understand these demons that combat veterans of PTSD share should put this on their must-read list. I thank God I have a friend like Bob who served alongside me and can so eloquently put into words the dark trench we combat veterans find ourselves in.

—David McCray, Section Chief for C Btry/4th/60th Artillery, C Btry/4th/60th Arty and E-41st Arty, 1st Field Force, Vietnam

A Civilian's Perspective

Robert Scholten—husband, father, minister, and soldier—was called to service in each role. Meeting him and learning of his various life experiences has been an honor. His humility and genuine commitment to his faith has encouraged me in working with the many veterans I encounter.

This book shares his recollections of the war he fought. Working with veterans, I have been humbled to learn of the unique experiences of each, yet the commonality of their emotions. Many have not been able to put to words these emotions as they struggle to escape the valley of pain they encountered. Robert has attempted to do so.

Giving voice to his recollections of his time in country, the dilemma of being a good soldier and a godly man is a lesson for veterans of every war. For Robert and his fellow soldiers there was no fanfare, just a silent landing and an attempt to resume his life stateside. He returned home with no resolution to the heartfelt desire to serve his country yet honor his faith. He has bared his soul, challenging each of us to serve our country and each other.

—Robert B. Woolley M.D. Psychiatrist,
Clinical PTSD Department and Clinical
PTSD In-House Program, Veterans Affairs
Hospital, Lexington, Kentucky

PREFACE

Be advised that this book is written as a journey. Please read it as such. Each chapter builds upon the previous one.

This book is written from within looking outward, not outward looking inward. You are about to view life from the perspective of PTSD.

Be thankful if the literary structure of this book seems choppy to you. It means the chances of you having PTSD are very unlikely. War changes people, some more than others. When thrown into combat, a person's entire being goes through a transformation that's faster than a blink of an eye. These transformations and their traumatic causes are the seedbed for Post Traumatic Stress Disorder. When this seedbed is ignored six or more months, PTSD takes root, slowly sending noxious runners throughout the host's entire being, eventually rewiring the brain and hijacking the nervous system. More is explained in the "Introduction to PTSD."

Be mindful that we with PTSD simultaneously live in the present and past. Also, we zone out as we zone in. In other words, we experience flashbacks without warning.

Be patient in this insight: PTSD can be likened to what the Bible describes as our "old and new nature" our "old and new self" our "old and new man." Read Appendix B for further insights into this comparison.

Be conscious of the fact that biblical principles in Psalm 25 are used to help bring some sense and meaning into a very misunderstood disorder. There are few people more misunderstood than war veterans afflicted with PTSD. Hopefully that will change.

INTRODUCTION TO POST TRAUMATIC STRESS DISORDER

In less than three seconds my wife's eyes fill with tears.

"Cheryl, are you okay?" my VA psychologist compassionately asks my wife of thirty-five years.

"Yes, I am."

Her once trickling tears now form streams flowing down her cheeks, meet on her chin, and from there drop into her lap.

Her lap—the very lap in which she lovingly rocked our infant daughters, that held her Bible from which she gained wisdom and strength beyond her years, that supported her folded hands in countless prayers, and upon which I rested my head gazing up into her deep brown eyes.

"Surprisingly, I am okay. I have hope now. For the first time I am beginning to understand things that have baffled me for years."

That is when the chip God chiseled off my reinforced bunkered life hits me square in the face.

"My God, how could I have hurt my wife so deeply for so long and not known it? Have I done the same thing to my daughters and my mother and others? I can't believe this. What has become of me?"

War! That is what became of me.

I thought I dealt with all this. But barricaded down deep in my heart were the forgotten "worst of the worst" memories of my life. They were securely imprisoned there during my tour of duty in Vietnam by my mind. Unbeknown to me, they had a secret ally named "time." And I was about to meet an escapee set free by "time."

On Wednesday, November 10, 2010, I slump in a chair across from my VA psychologist as I have done every Wednesday morning for nearly a year.

"What do you have there, Robert?" she asks, referring to a crumpled piece of paper in my right hand.

Slowly I raise my head to make eye contact with her. A smile greets me, along with expressive eyes hoping to finally see signs of a breakthrough. I sense her hope just as she senses my dread of proceeding.

Frustrated and annoyed, I try reading the note, but nothing comes out. Slumping forward, I nearly fall out of the chair.

"Robert, take a deep breath. Then take your time reading."

"I received the first draft of my book, *Psalm 25 & PTSD*."

"That is great. What an accomplishment!"

Snapping upward I speak out, "No, it is not. It's terrible. But you won't think so. In fact, you will agree with this editorial note."

While slowly unfolding my editor's note, I lose all concept of time until being brought back by Dr. Dee swiveling her office chair. She knows from years of experience not to startle a veteran by sudden or loud noises.

"I don't want to read this" keeps throbbing in my head, keeping perfect rhythm with my rising blood pressure. This is unfair and unjust and unwanted...and it is...right and true. Taking three or four deep breaths I begin reading the note:

"While this introduction does set up present events nicely, I'm looking for more background information. Why is your story different? What will endear you to readers? Including a memory of actually being in battle would draw readers in emotionally and set the stage nicely for you to begin discussing your purpose for the book. It will be an immediate hook for readers, which is essential."

"Dr Dee, she's asking me to do the impossible."

"No, Robert. She is not."

"Yes, she is," I snap back. "I have spent the last forty years avoiding, denying, bushwhacking, and pushing back what she wants brought forth."

"She is right, you know."

Throwing my weight backward into the chair, I raise my arms in frustration while taking several deep breaths. "I know. I know. I know you both are right. But it doesn't make it any easier."

"Dig deep, Robert. Dig deep and hard. Keep digging till you reach those memories; then bring one to light. The associated emotions and feelings will follow."

"That's what I'm afraid of. I don't know how I'll react. Nor do I know how my family will handle all this."

"Yes, you do. Remember Cheryl and her tears?"

My thoughts immediately flash back to mid-October, when God took a hammer and chisel to chip away at my reinforced bunkered life. What a strange combination of tools he used—but very effective: the hammer was my VA psychologist and the chisel my wife. Powerless against the Master Redeemer's skillful hands, I watched a chip fly into my face. It was a chip I'll remember for the rest of my life.

Dr. Dee, after months of work, wasn't going to let this tiny breakthrough get by her; nor by me.

"Robert; is it okay for me to invite Cheryl in to discuss this together?"

"Yes, I suppose so."

"You suppose so?"

After taking a deep breath I agree. Uncertainty: is this the feeling? If so, I don't like it. While still in thought, my precious wife enters the room to quietly sit in the chair beside mine.

Dr Dee addresses her with a gentle soft voice, "I believe we have a breakthrough this morning. It is an important one, and Bob has agreed it would be good to bring you in on it."

Cheryl shifts herself slightly toward me as I raise my head and straighten my posture in the chair, wishing I could simply disappear in it.

Our eyes meet. I remember when such contacts melted my heart and thrilled my soul, bringing hope and joy to the moment and beyond. Now there is nothing. My heart sinks further into misery. I can't take much more of this!

"Cheryl…you know I love you."

I couldn't go any further. I was starting to shut down to avoid…"O God, help me; please help me. I've got to do this," bursts from my soul as a prayer; a last-ditch prayer.

"Cheryl, Dr. Dee has brought something to my attention. And I just can't get my mind around it. She says that somewhere in Vietnam I shut down my emotions in order to survive the madness of war and that I have been void of them since. That's not true, is it?"

In less than three seconds her eyes fill with tears.

"Robert, what are you feeling right now?" Dr. Dee gently asks.

"Nothing; I know I ought too. But I don't."

"Cheryl, are you okay?" Dr. Dee compassionately asks my wife of thirty-five years.

"Yes, I am. Surprisingly, I have hope now. For the first time I am beginning to understand things that have baffled me for years." As she speaks, her once trickling tears form streams flowing down her cheeks, meeting on her chin, and drop into her lap.

That is when the chip God chiseled off my reinforced bunkered life hits me square in the face.

"My God, how could I have hurt my wife so deeply for so long and not known it? Have I done this to my daughters and my mother and others? I can't believe this. What has become of me?"

Thus one of the haunting effects of PTSD in the lives of war combatants: numbness.

Memory lapses of time spent in war are another common effect of PTSD.

There are time lapses in my memory of Vietnam. But now, forty years later, my mind is ever so slowly dislodging some of those memories through persistent therapy from VA PTSD clinical team members. Once dislodged, we work through the harsh issues that drive my mind to deeply bury them in the first place.

"It was buried for a reason," I tell myself while wrestling with my assignment to write about a combat experience.

Sitting on a couch in my basement, I rock myself in a back and forth motion, trying to remember and forget at the same time. Slowly my rocking motion speeds up to two rocks per second as my world shrinks to a circular five inches with a crosshair in the middle.

"To your right...your right...twenty yards out," becomes louder and louder as I rock on the edge of the couch, oblivious to my surroundings. "'RPG'...'RPG' twenty yards out!" our squad leader yells while frantically helping cannoneers feed our forty-millimeter cannons four-round clips every two to three seconds. (RPG - Rocket Propelled Grenade)

My ears and head throb as I sit in the gunner's seat of my Duster in the Central Highlands of war-torn Vietnam. All around me is organized chaos as our five man crew works in split second rhythm defiantly fighting off death while sending deadly fire back towards the advancing Viet Cong.

There's no time to think about death or life when catapulted into combat–you simply fight with every fiber of your being as your body saturates itself with super charged chemicals.

Around us are the sounds of war as small arm projectiles join machinegun rounds ricocheting off our thinly armored tub (open turret) while others pass between and over us. This joins our 40mm cannons returning fire at 2 rounds per second and our mounted M60 machinegun spitting out hundreds of bullets per minute.

My world has now shrunk to a small one-inch crosshair in the middle of the site before me as our crew walks high explosive anti-aircraft projectiles toward their target. Disregarding the sound of bullets hitting around and passing by me, as do my fellow crew members, I watch as an RPG-toting Viet Cong comes into my one-inch world. He fires first, missing us by inches. I fire second, watching two highly explosive forty-millimeter projectiles hit their mark chest-high, exploding into thousands of pieces of flack-metal.

There is no time to react as more RPGs and mortars are zeroing in on our position. Additional Duster personnel and infantry join in cracking open ammo canisters, passing up forty-millimeter clips as fast as they can. Our five-man crew has grown to over a dozen. More are needed as additional troops frantically lug metal ammo canisters of forty-millimeter rounds through enemy fire to our Duster.

Then it happens—a blinding flash of light and an earth-shattering noise followed by a pounding concussion filled with dirt, rock, sand, and shrapnel. "How could they miss us at such close range?" I yell, falling backward into the couch in the basement of my home in southeastern Kentucky on Monday, November 15, 2010.

Flashbacks—unwanted, terrifying, and all too real— are another symptom of PTSD, one that we war veterans avoid like the plague. We all came through that death-defying experience back in the spring of 1971 without a scratch. Unbelievable but true. All too true again for me.

Post-traumatic Stress Disorder is nothing new; it is actually ancient. It is as old as war itself.

In the past it has been called by various names such as: shell shock, battle fatigue, and a soldier's heart, to name a few. To my knowledge, it wasn't until after the Vietnam War that serious studies and research slowly started yielding insights into the effects of war, especially combat, upon the whole being of a veteran. What they found was just a small crack of insight in the massive door that held back centuries of heartache, pain, sorrow, and fear tightly intertwined in compounded layers of anguish.

We human beings, with our indwelling souls, carry war's negative and positive life-changing experiences into the future. In so doing, we weave war's seen and unseen effects into the very fabrics of our families, communities, and societies.

I'm rewired" was an unwanted fact I learned back in November and December of 2007 during my six weeks in the Lexington, Kentucky's Veterans Affairs In-House Clinical PTSD Rehabilitation Program.

During combat, my body responded to heightened stresses by producing supercharged chemicals (two of which are adrenalin and noradrenalin), firing them straight to the brain. In turn, my brain instantly fired messages to all the organs and nerves to fight or flight or freeze. If fight, to do so with every fiber of my being, disregarding my own well being for my well being and that of my fellow comrades in arms.[1]

To complicate things further, we PTSD veterans get hooked on these legal self-induced drugs, to our detriment.

If you are scratching your head right about now, be sure to thank the good Lord. Why? Such action doesn't make a lick of sense unless you have personally experienced the insanity of warfare.

Staying alive in violent situations often means moving fast, getting violent yourself, staying alert, not sleeping, and not allowing attention to be taken up with trivial things. This "neural hijacking" continues into civilian life, responding to such things as loud or sudden noises, smells, and sudden movements caught by the corner of the eye.[2]

I'm tired and worn out from trying to finish this portion of the Introduction, which is now six days overdue. At best, I'll finish it by tonight. I have to. I must, and I will get it completed before I go to sleep.

Thus, another aspect of PTSD is PTG, post-traumatic growth. PTG is the development of highly positive characteristics brought about by the traumatic events that are the seedbeds of Post Traumatic Stress Disorder.[3]

I have been living with PTG for decades. However, until recently I did not know what to call it. For decades now I have been telling people that my time in Vietnam (life-altering experiences) enabled me to accomplish difficult tasks. At the age of twenty-two, I embarked upon a successful eight-year quest to obtain both a bachelor and master's degree. Now for the rest of the story! I could barely read or write upon my entrance into college.

Is there such a thing as PTG? You bet there is. And I thank God for it. But that PTG wouldn't be present in my life apart from PTSD. Can I say thank you? Yes, in a very humble way.[4]

INTRODUCTION TO
PSALM 25 & PTSD

Hanging up the phone one late afternoon, I whisper, "What am I doing? God, I hope calling the VA is the right thing to do. If it isn't, please block it, Lord. Please do not let it come about."

Time marches on, but for me it is reduced to a snail's pace as I wait on the VA's decision. During this waiting game, I pray: *Lord God Almighty, what is happening to me? I dealt with all this stuff years ago. This cannot be happening to me. What will I do? What will I say? What will people think?*

Answering the phone in our bedroom one midmorning, I nearly die when realizing it is the clinical PTSD department of the Lexington VA hospital calling. As the gentleman identifies himself and the purpose of his call, I want to hang up in his ear or, better yet, drop the receiver and run for my life.

The phone call is only to last fifteen to twenty minutes. It has now gone on well over thirty minutes with no signs of letting up. I long since closed our bedroom door, as I do not want Cheryl, my wife, to hear me answering all these questions.

One thing's for sure: I am getting my exercise by pacing back and forth while trying to remain calm and doing my best not to run.

"Mr. Scholten. Mr. Scholten, are you still there? Robert. Mr. Scholten. Robert. Robert..."

I close my eyes, trying to block everything out. In opening them, I am not ready to see what I am looking into.

I walk myself into a corner, placing my forehead smack dab in the middle of it.

It was that question that did this to me!

God, I can't answer this. I just cannot, Lord. Oh God, I'm afraid of what you are having me do. What am I doing? I ask myself with no intention of answering. In my soul the awaiting answer is, *I am reaching out for help.* In my heart the awaiting answer is, *Run, you fool.* In my mind, the awaiting answer is, *There must be another way around this.* During all this, God must be looking down on me, smiling. He knows my appointed time is about to begin, taking me with it into the future one day at a time.

"Mr. Scholten, are you still with me?"

"Yes."

"Are you okay?"

"I do not know. I just don't know how to answer that. I guess I'm not...Oh Lord, help me."

"Mr. Scholten, you still have not answered my question. Mr. Scholten. Robert. Robert..."

Opening my eyes again, I find myself back in that same corner, doing the same thing I was previously doing: denying what I know has to be answered and confessed.

"Mr. Scholten, are you thinking about harming yourself? Mr. Scholten. Robert."

"No. Not right now. Yes, I have thought about taking myself out." Plopping my head back into the corner, I pray, *Oh Lord, now I've done it. Oh God. No one is going to understand. How do I tell my family about all this?*

While still listening and responding to the man from the VA, I pray silently, *I want to run, Lord. I want to run again. Keep me here, Lord. Help me face this. You know my heart. Oh God, help me face this, for I cannot go through it alone.*

Upon the completion of the phone conversation, I hang up the receiver in disbelief of what just took place. Down deep in my soul I know this is being arranged by my gracious God who loves me even though I fought in Vietnam.

———————

Another phone call at another time, I receive the information that frightens me more than anything else: my acceptance into the Lexington VA hospital's PTSD clinical in-house program.

———————

I am fighting a losing battle against God's Spirit, which is nudging me ever so gently and persistently toward my appointed time with the VA. I fight up to the day. I fight throughout that day. I fight through the first week and then the second, third, and the fourth weeks.

Finally, with some additional help, I am able to draw something out of the fifth week and a little more out of the sixth week. Sadly, being true to my Nam nature, I do not remember any names of my fellow veterans from those six weeks.

By looking back on those six weeks within the timeline of the previous four decades, it becomes obvious that that help was way overdue.

Another observation is that we who suffer with PTSD view time differently from those who do not. My view of time is set within the ten traumatic months in war-torn Vietnam.

Vietnam for me is not something that happened four decades ago. It is yesterday turning into today, in which Vietnam is fully alive within me. This is a constant frustration I wrestle with, as do millions upon millions of other veterans who fought in wars.

Everything changes, so it seems, once you survive war, be you a veteran or be you a civilian caught up in its insanity or be you a loved one of such survivors. My mother, Grace, was such a person. The war I fought in she also fought at home, as did so many other parents and loved ones of Nam vets. It was alive in my mother and was so right up to her deathbed, from which she said, "Robert, no one will ever know what I went through those ten months you were in Vietnam. Every day since, I have thanked God for bringing you home safely. Now I pray for all our boys in Iraq and Afghanistan."

My mother carried Nam for nearly forty years, as have I. She passed from this world to her heavenly reward, leaving behind a long-fought battle, a battle not of her own making but forced upon her when she daringly rose up in its face to pray me through it. Not all mothers' prayers were or are answered in a fashion such as hers were. She was aware of that and was praying for such moms all the days of her life.

I once wrote, "War is likened unto salvation. Once you experience it, your life is never the same."[5] I stand by that even more so now than I did back in 1988.

According to the Bible, there is an appointed time for everything under heaven. Part of this appointed time is war, just as it is of peace. Another biblical insight into our times, as in times past, is the ever-present wars and rumors of wars.

When writing what we know as Ecclesiastes 3:1–8, King Solomon must have looked back on his father, King David's, life:

> To everything there is a season, a time for every purpose under heaven: a time to be born, and a time to die; a time to plant, and a time to pluck what is planted; a time to kill, and a time to heal; a time to break down, and a time to build up; a time to weep, and a time to laugh; a time to mourn, and a time to dance; a time to cast away stones, and a time to gather stones; a time to embrace, and a time to refrain from embracing; a time to gain, and a time to lose; a time to keep, and a time to throw away; a time to tear, and a time to sew; a time to keep silenced, and a time to speak; a time to love; and a time to hate; a time of war, and a time of peace.
>
> Ecclesiastics 3:1–8

You are about to embark upon a journey few of us war veterans allow anyone entrance to.

That journey for me began when I came down on levy for Vietnam. I did not ask to go. I did not volunteer to go. I did not wish to go. But I went because it was the thing to do as a soldier in the United States Army.

I survived boot camp at Fort Jackson, South Carolina. I swatted mosquitoes in AIT (combat engineer, water purification) at Fort Leonard Wood, Missouri. I had the time of my life driving M60 tanks at Fort Hood, Texas. I had the worst time of my life on a government-sponsored tour of Vietnam. I closed out my hitch in the army at Fort Bliss, Texas.

Unbeknown to me, I picked something up in Vietnam that seemingly laid dormant for many long years, before its symptoms broke out in my life. It left me for dead. That is how I felt when it unleashed itself in my life, bursting out into my family, and beyond.

Walk with me now into *PSALM 25 & PTSD*. Some place within its written pages my journey will become your journey. I do not know when your individual journey will begin; but you will. Think about keeping a journal in which you can write your thoughts. By the time you reach the final chapter your journal may be full.

PROLOGUE

You and I begin our journey together by reading "*A Warrior's Prayer*" that was written by King David. It is Psalm 25. Special to me are these twenty-two verses filled with encouragement, hope, comfort, peace, and strength. This psalm has been an ever-present friend and guide through my life since 1966 when I put it to memory.

I never dreamed that one day, forty-four years of meditation and study and applications of Psalm 25 would be woven into the forty years of post-Vietnam (PTSD) living. But the good Lord, through his mercy and endless nudging in my life, did just that. It is my prayer that both you and I will benefit from that mosaic of faith, hope and love. [6]

> *To You, O Lord, I lift up my soul. O my God, I trust in You; let me not be ashamed; let not my enemies triumph over me. Indeed, let no one who waits on You be ashamed; let those be ashamed who deal treacherously without cause. Show me Your ways, O Lord; teach me Your paths. Lead me in Your truth and teach me, for You are the God of my salvation; on You do I wait all the day. Remember, O Lord, Your tender mercies and Your lovingkindnesses, for*

they are from of old. Do not remember the sins of my youth, nor my transgressions; according to Your mercy remember me, for Your goodness' sake, O Lord. Good and upright is the Lord; therefore He teaches sinners in the way. The humble He guides in justice, and the humble He teaches His way. All the paths of the Lord are mercy and truth, to such as keep His covenant and His testimonies. For Your name's sake, O Lord, pardon my iniquity, for it is great. Who is the man who fears the Lord? Him shall He teach in the way He chooses. He himself shall dwell in prosperity, and his descendents shall inherit the earth. The secret of the Lord is with those who fear Him, and He will show them His covenant. My eyes are ever toward the Lord, for He shall pluck my feet out of the net. Turn Yourself to me, and have mercy upon me, for I am desolate and afflicted. The troubles of my heart have enlarged; bring me out of my distress! Look upon my affliction and my pain, and forgive all my sins. Consider my enemies, for they are many; and they hate me with cruel hatred. Keep my soul, and deliver me; let me not be ashamed, for I put my trust in You. Let integrity and uprightness preserve me, for I trust in You. Redeem Israel, O God, out of all their troubles.

Psalm 25

Within the pages to follow, you will not find written discourses on the verses of Psalm 25. Hopefully you will experience the heartfelt expressions of hope flowing through its time-tested principles into your heart and life.

LIFTING UP MY SOUL

To you, O Lord, I lift up my soul.

I'm stuck and know not what to do. Feelings of abandonment overwhelm me in this lonely existence of daily struggles with affliction. God, my God, how did I end up here? I know how just as I know what to do. But such knowledge that served me so well in decades past has become a battleground from which I must experience eternal truths.

I've been here before. This I know. The terrain is different, but the trail is not. This God-forsaken place seems much more miserable if it is the same place. My heart tries to convince me we are elsewhere, while my soul pleads for mercy and truth. Which do I believe? This I also know.

Oh God, my God, to Thee, O Lord, I lift up my soul. My soul is heavy and weary as I gaze upon this path with so many footsteps imbedded in it. So many footsteps. How can they be distinguished? Which do I follow? My mind is overwhelmed, my heart is suffering, my soul is yearning, and my life is at a standstill in this dreadful place I despise.

Stuck and unable to find an escape, I try turning backward. But my feet are stuck in this path, so I twist to look backward only to see the impenetrable blackness of emptiness.

"Do not look backwards but forwards, for therein lies your destiny" flows through me like a sharp sword, a doubled-edged sword.[7]

Looking downward at the path, two things become obvious to me: my shoes are not appropriate for this place, and all the footprints are facing forward.[8] *What else?* slips out from deep in my heart. *Do not answer that, Lord. I don't want to know,* leaps from my mind into my heart and out my mouth, echoing off eternity.

This path has been worn deep by the feet of countless people who have fallen into this forsaken place or were gently placed here. Either way, they faced the same challenge awaiting me: "unto Thee."

I do not want to be here. I want out, barely finished forming in my mind when I heard, "Welcome, Robert. Your appointed time has opened up before you. Fret not. Neither worry, for you are not alone."

Yeah right! I do not see anyone or anything but this path and that only inches before me.

Somewhere from the darkness a soothing voice states, "You are ready."

My instant reply is, "No, I am not. Nor will I ever be."

Standing motionless, I feel and hear my beating heart as though my chest is about to burst wide open. Blood vessels in my head join in with a pounding that makes my ears hurt.

If only I could wish myself out of this place.

What a desperately naive thought. I cannot wish myself out of here any more than pray myself out. This I know all too well from experience and the Bible, God's Word. I have to pass through here, for God placed me here and has given me sufficient grace to handle everything that comes my way.[9] Trust, obedience, perseverance, proven character, hope, and faith are about to do battle with distrustfulness, disobedience, impatience, self-centeredness, hopelessness, doubt, and disbelief.

Here I stand in a battleground of conflicting wills, desires, and wants. The longer I remain stationary, the more intense the battle becomes within and around me.

I know from past experience in this dark and appalling place that I must give in, yield, surrender, forfeit my will and desires and wants to those of the Lord. *Who does he think he is anyway to do with me as he pleases?* is a silent thought of mine.[10]

"Mine," shatters the silence and startles me outright. "You are mine."[11]

Now what have I done? I know better, yet I still challenge him who knows me best. Here, right here where hope meets hopelessness, faith meets faithlessness, fearlessness meets fearfulness, courage meets discouragement, goodness meets badness, righteousness meets unrighteousness, and truth meets falseness.

Unto thee, not unto me is easier said than done. It is right here in "unto thee" situations in life, anywhere in life, and anytime in life that I and every other human being, Christian or non-Christian, face our mortality.

Unto thee is an acknowledgment of my mortality and a confession of my need for divine intervention.

From "unto thee" to "O Lord" is a long, treacherous leap that proves or disproves my determination to follow through on previous vows of commitment to Jesus's lordship over my life and lifestyle. "O Lord" is the center of life for all life in this life here on earth. "O Lord" is a way of life into which I have been placed by the sovereign actions of God.

TRUST IS AN ISSUE

O my God, I trust in You; let me not be ashamed;
let not my enemies triumph over me.

O my God, you are God, the One and Only true God.
This I believe and confess publically.[12] Yet there are times
when I raise my eyes heavenward, bend my knees upon
this ground, and lift my voice unto you not in confidence
but in soul-searching questions.

What's happening to me, Lord? What's happening?
Oh my God, in you I trust. Who else do I have?

I do not understand. Or do I not want to understand?
Is the truth I fear the truth? Fear is a fearful thing, especially
when it is feared. My God, I am living in a vicious circle.

Who could ever truly understand such a predica-
ment? My family. My precious family has been trying and
has refused to give up on me as they conquer one defen-
sive wall at a time only to find another.

I can identify with the Apostle Paul when he says,
"Wretched man that I am! Who will set me free from the
body of this death?" (Romans 7:24, NASB).

"Thanks be to God through Jesus Christ our Lord!"[13]
Yes. God the Father. I trust and love him, and I adore and
love his Son, Jesus, my Savior.

This is where another ongoing struggle has entrenched itself in my life: that of love, trust, and obedience doing battle with tolerance, distrust, and disobedience. I am loved by the Creator of the universe. I have been so since before the foundations of the world.[14]

As a Christian, I am commanded in the Word of God to love and accept love, to forgive and accept forgiveness, to be merciful and accept mercy, to encourage and accept encouragement, to enter into a person's anguish to assist him through it and accept another person's assistance to help me through my anguish, even that which is entrenched, fiercely defended, and booby-trapped against all intruders.

If I trust the Lord and love him, I must also trust those he sends into my life as ambassadors of his kingdom, of which I am a member, a rebellious member. My God, is this true? Yes. The thought of it disgusts and hurts me. But my defense mechanisms and offensive battlements are shielding me all too well.

All the excuses, justifications, and reasons for my rebellious behavior are invalid before God Almighty. I know this fact, but that hasn't stopped me from trying. Thank God I am fighting a losing war of wits. I can never outwit the Lord. No one has or will ever outwit God. That is good news to my ears.

For me to think about making up excuses for my less-than-righteous behavior is shameful. To actually lay an excuse before the Lord, trying to justify my actions against him and his ways, is downright dangerous.

I have been there, done that, and paid for it. The payments for such actions have been the same down through the ages: painful and shameful.

Adam and Eve found out the hard way. The pain and shame they brought upon themselves (and upon humanity) was so great that it took two generations before their descendants sought God in prayer.[15]

Oh Lord my God, I have come a long way in accepting responsibility for my actions against you. And I admit there's still a long journey before me.

I fully understand and identify with King David's request, for mine is the same. I trust in you, Lord. Let me not be ashamed, nor let me be put to shame by those who pattern their lives after this world.

Living life as it ought to be is getting harder day by day. It's so much easier to go astray than to stay on the way of the Lord. Help me, Jesus, for I trust in you. Please do not let my enemies of doubt, anger, mistrust, anxiousness, and the like triumph over me.[16]

Enemies are kept at bay or fought off or outright eliminated by good guards. I confess to being a lousy guard of my heart and mind. My best efforts often fall short, thus exposing myself to assaults from the enemy of my soul.[17]

What do I do? What I should have done in the first place: trust the appointed guard over my life and soul and mind, as explained in Philippians 4:6–7:

> Be anxious for nothing, but in everything by prayer and supplication, with thanksgiving, let your requests be made known to God; and the peace of God, which surpasses all understanding, will guard your hearts and minds through Christ Jesus.

When will I learn?

WAITING IS HARD TO DO

Indeed, let no one who waits on You be ashamed;
let those be ashamed who deal treacherous without cause.

Oh Lord God, be patient with me as you give me more patience. How asinine of a request. God has already given me more than enough patience and faith to face whatever life throws at me, just as he has everyone else he calls unto himself through his Son, Jesus.[18]

My request of him must be, "Help me, Lord, to be patient, for I find it all too easy to be impatient," and, "Help me trust you as I wait upon you this very moment of this very hour of this very day of my life."

That's accountability. I do not like that word either, but how I thank God for it. Marriages are held together by it, as are nations. Journalists are kept honest by it, as are politicians. Military personnel's actions are kept just and merciful by it, as are civilians.'

Where there is no accountability, marriages start falling apart from within, as do nations. Journalists become self-serving, as do politicians. Military personnel become ruthless, as do civilians.

I had to learn the value and purpose of waiting upon the Lord God Almighty. It did not come easy or quickly. Because I wanted it my way rather than thy way, thus thy had to reshape me on his spinning potter's wheel.[19] I have been dizzy most my life. I still am at times, especially now.

Now. Yes, now. I'm stuck in the present moment in this darkened realm of PTSD. It is here that yesterdays yesterday's play havoc with today.

Day by day, I hope to escape into tomorrow by outrunning today. My days have been invaded by the long, treacherous tentacles of a war once fought but never ending. It is here in this terrible place I am striving to live a life pleasing unto God.

How long must I wait before you deliver me? Herein is another daily challenge of believing that God has a purpose for me being here rather than where I want to be: out of here.

Anywhere but here, Lord. Please, anywhere but here.

Have I been reduced to such weakness of character and resolve that I have given up on him who knows me best and loves me most and has more confidence in me than I have in myself? No, I haven't. So what's happening to me, Lord? How and why do you put up with me?[20]

I know all the answers. They are found in my heart and in heaven above, sitting at the right side of God the Father Almighty. He is my hope in this seemingly hopeless condition I find myself in. He is the solid foundation in these shifting times of uncertainty.

The answer is not found in the blowing of the wind but in the heartfelt writings of an ancient warrior who fought battles on battlefields, on the home front (in his home), and in his personal heart and life, all his life. King David was his name. And Psalm 23 is his fame.

The Lord is my shepherd; I shall not want. He maketh me to lie down in green pastures: He leadeth me beside the still waters. He restoreth my soul: he leadeth me in the paths of righteousness for his name's sake. Yea, though I walk through the valley of the shadow of death, I will fear no evil: for thou art with me; thy rod and staff they comfort me. Thou prepareth a table before me in the presence of mine enemies: thou anointest my head with oil; my cup runneth over. Surely goodness and mercy shall follow me all the days of my life; and I will dwell in the house of the Lord forever.

Psalm 23 (KJV)

Jesus, another Shepherd and King, calls me to come to him just as I am, weary to the point of exhaustion.

"Come to me, all ye who labor and are heavy laden, and I will give you rest. Take My yoke upon you, and learn from Me; for I am gentle and lowly in heart: and you will find rest for your souls. For My yoke is easy, and My burden is light."[21]

Exhausted, that I am. I feel as though my life is a burden, a burden I have been carrying *since facing the truth about war: it is life changing for all my life.*

Some changes are for the good in the long run, but there is the dark side few wish to reveal, let alone talk about or, worse yet, remember. Remembrance opens doors long sealed against intruders and concealed from prying eyes, including compassionate eyes and concerned hearts and open minds, seeking understanding in order to help a loved one or friend in need.

There are times I am my worst enemy. How can this be? Simple. All too easily, I've learned with deadly accuracy, how to keep people from penetrating my secured perimeter. When I stand guard over my heart and mind, no one gets through because everyone is seen as an intruder who wants to dismantle my security system. That isn't going to happen.

Eventually I cry out to the Lord from that bunker when its hardened walls come in on me, squeezing out what life and hope I have left, so it seems. The truth is my hope is secure, as is my life, because neither are mine. They belong to the Shepherd King, who is the rightful guardian of my soul.[22]

From within the darkness that shrouds me, like a damp wool blanket, my heart hears the Lord calling me unto himself to comfort me, encourage me, and reassure me of his enduring presence even here, this very moment.[23]

"Robert, your every need is being met. You have nothing to worry about. Everything has been taken care of for you. Believe it. Then proceed forward one step at a time."[24]

"What? One step at a time! I'll never get out of here."

"And if you do not, will you still love me and trust me and follow me?"

"Yes, Lord. I will."

"Then move forward, for you are not alone. Nor will you ever be."

It is here in these brief moments of clarity that I declare:

> To You, O Lord, I lift up my soul. O my God, I trust in You; let me not be ashamed; let not my enemies triumph over me. Indeed, let no one who waits on You be ashamed; let those be ashamed who deal treacherously without cause.[25]
>
> Psalm 25:1–3

TO LEARN OR NOT TO LEARN

Show me Your ways, O Lord; Teach me Your paths.

I'm ready to move forward, Lord. But my heart and mind are in conflict with each other, which makes me jittery. I know you are present. I know that I have been claimed by you. And I know that all things will work together for my good because I love you and because you called me according to your purpose for me.[26]

But I'm still in this lousy place. I still cannot see light at either end of this pitiful valley. And I hate this place and everything in it.

I guess I'm not ready. Subconsciously, I want to stomp my feet in protest against being sentenced to a life saturated by and shrouded in PTSD. It's an injustice, I tell you. My blood pressure is rising, as is my anger. My hope is dissipating, as is my will to survive.

Oh God, help me, for I cannot survive in this place apart from you. Forgive me for straining my eyes by looking intently into the darkness, hoping to see a glimmer of light rather than finding my hope in your Word, which is a light unto my feet, as I walk by faith, not by sight, on the path in which you placed me.[27]

This path, despised by so many and cherished by none, had its beginning just outside the garden of Eden. Who could ever know the unbearable pain Adam and Eve felt upon being cast out of Eden? God did. Not that he sinned, but that he loved the very first sinners of all.

Right there at the outside of Eden's gate a new path awaited the fallen royal couple. Theirs were the first footprints on this pitiful pathway that has come to be known as the valley of the shadow of death.

The first footsteps of these two disgraced, grief-stricken, fear-struck, guilt-laden people paved the way for the rest of us. Since then, countless people have struggled in this shadowy valley with intense feelings of fear and doubt wrapped up in cloaks of uncertainties.

As I walk through this darkened trench of PTSD, a slender beam of light illuminating from beneath my feet guides me. That precious light is from the Word of God, for which I am thankful.[28] I would be hopeless in this discouraging place without it.

Here I kneel on my knees, with head bowed in remorse, arms lifted in reverence. This intense internal struggle of wills is temporally brought to an end by meditating on Scriptures.

> I beseech you therefore, brethren, by the mercies of God, that you present your bodies a living sacrifice, holy, acceptable to God, which is your reasonable service. And do not be conformed to this world, but be transformed by the renewing of your mind, that you may prove what is that good and acceptable and perfect will of God.
>
> Romans 12:1–2

This freed me to cry out, "Make me know your ways, oh Lord. Teach me your paths."

Your is the key. It is all about God's ways and paths, not mine. God's ways are perfect, while mine are imperfect and a crime against him.[29]

"Make me" is the plea. It is all about submitting to God's authority over me. After all, he did create me.[30]

"Make me know Your ways" is the fee. It is costly to know the ways of the Lord as Jesus would have me know them. That is because to know them is to do them. Anything less than delighting myself in the ways of the Lord is a conflict of interests. [31]

This is not my first struggle of wills, nor will it be the last. I'm hoping they will decrease in number and in intensity and in time. I know how to bring these improvements about. Just acknowledging that makes me anxious.

"Oh God, my God, you are my one and only hope. Help me keep my mind and eyes open to your will so I can identify your ways, which are perfect and altogether lovely. Please also help me maintain a teachable heart so I can learn your paths."[32]

Some of these pathways lead to faith, hope, and love. God's gift of faith is fortified in his Word. The hope from above is anchored securely in his sovereign will.

And the unadulterated love flowing from God's heavenly throne is my eternal security.[33]

"Show me your ways, oh Lord, for they all have been proven true down through the ages.

They are trustworthy and altogether perfect, even here in this dark, dreary place."[34]

RUNNING TO OR FROM THE TRUTH

Lead me in Your truth and teach me, For You
are the God of my salvation; On You do I wait
all the day.

"Show me that again. Again! Another time, please. I need
to see that one more time. Just once more."

"How did you do that?"

"Good grief! How many times do I have to show you,
anyway?"

"I'm sorry; I just can't get it."

"Will you pay attention?"

"I am."

"Well then, one more time."

"Thank you."

"There! Do you get it now?"

Some lessons are very hard to learn. Some are seemingly impossible. Thankfully, others are mastered in a
snap.

"Lead me in your truth and teach me." It doesn't get
any more basic than that.

Lead me, Lord, and I will follow. Teach me, Lord, and I will learn. That sounds simple enough. Then why do I not follow him more closely? And why do I not enthusiastically hang on to every word of his Word?

The basic truth is that I'm running from the truth more than I'm running to it, and that running is wearing me out. Besides, it is hard enough walking in this treacherous place, let alone running.

So why am I running? What am I running from? And to where am I running? These are heart issues needing honest answers. To bring forth such answers, I need to face myself in the mirror of God's Word, the Holy Bible. In order to do such a thing I need to pray, "Lead me, Lord, in Your truth. And teach me, for You are the God of my salvation. On You I wait all the day."[35]

Do I really want to go forward with this? My soul yearns for me to do so. My mind questions the ramifications of it all. And my heart is at war between the old and new natures within me.

War is a fact of life I know all too well. It sets me apart from those who have not experienced its madness and insanity. It sets me in motion on a journey for which I was unprepared. And it starts an internal clock I was unaware of.

I left Vietnam, but Vietnam never left me. Nam hitched a ride in my heart and hijacked my life.

I had no idea what awaited me after my tour of duty in Vietnam. I stepped out of one war right into another. Sadly, millions took that same step. Those millions need to be multiplied to include family members and friends who were shanghaied.

What a journey! Nearly forty years of inching my way through this endless trench has been more than enough. *God, it has been enough, hasn't it?* I know the answer. So why wait for it? Forgive me, Lord, for I know better.

I'm not alone, but it sure feels that way. There are others here. There have to be. I momentarily stand motionless, eventually sighing, only to hear it fading into infinity.

As silence overtakes the echo I murmur, "This much I've learned. There is a deeply worn rut in the bottom of the valley of the shadow of death where light never penetrates and the air seems stagnant. It's down here you find Post Traumatic Stress Disorder. It is also where you will find me. I never dreamed in my wildest nightmares I would end up here."

I take a deep breath, holding it until my lungs hurt, before releasing it with a defiant shout: "But here I am!"

"Oh, what's the use?"

Lord, my Savior and constant companion, I'm not giving up on you. That I will never do. It's me, Lord. It's me I am ready to give up on.

From a distance I faintly hear what seems to be a gentle breeze. Still standing motionless, I hear it coming closer. Leaning forward with eyes closed, head tilted slightly upward, and arms reaching outward as to embrace a long-lost friend, I wait.

I lose myself in thoughts of yesteryear only to have them yield to the reality of this place. But still I wait, now patiently.

Wait a minute. There are more sounds.

"Yes, there are," I tell myself.

I'm beginning to hear footsteps.

"Oh, God. I'm not alone."

MERCY. DO I DESERVE IT?

Remember, O Lord, Your tender mercies and Your loving kindnesses, For they are from of old.

"Here I am, Lord. Come get me. I am ready to be rescued."

Closer. I can now feel the gentle breeze caressing my stiff face and tense body, penetrating my very soul. "Oh God, how sweet is your Spirit and how glorious is your presence. You refresh me; you restore my hope; you strengthen my resolve."[36]

"What did I just say? You strengthen my what? My resolve? For what are you strengthening it?

"To continue," comes the answer I do not want to hear.

"Remember to remember who you are and to whom you belong and with whom you will spend eternity."

Standing silent in the presence of God's Spirit, I dare not say or think anything. Just moments before, I yearned for God's touch by means of his Holy Spirit. Now I stand shivering with layers of goose bumps over my body.

My mind is working double-time trying to find appropriate scriptural verses for this encounter I'm having, much like Abraham and Moses.[37] My heart is melting. My body is fully alive, as is my spirit. My soul is like a sponge in a fisherman's hand, who slowly releases his grip, allowing water to saturate every spore and fiber of the once-living sea creature.

Basking in the presence of the Lord, I lose all sense of time, which is mighty fine with me because nothing else matters. Slowly but steadily, Bible verses come to mind, which I turn into prayers to take with me. "Have mercy, Lord. Have mercy upon me. Remember your tender mercies and compassion, for I cannot survive without them."

"Oh Lord, I rejoice in your mercy and compassion of old. They, like you, are the same yesterday, today, and tomorrow.[38]

Oh my God, as you were to King David, you are with me, faithful and true.[39]

So I humbly stand before you with a true grateful heart and a broken spirit,[40] both having been conquered by your Word.

"Heavenly Father, I have fallen into your righteous hands in which my life resembles a speck.[41]

Who am I that you care for me?"[42]

"Oh Lord my God, I know that soon, very soon, all too soon, your Holy Spirit will nudge me out of this sacred moment and guide me further into…I cannot even get myself to say it, Lord."[43]

"God, I feel like King Jehoshaphat when the entire Aramean army was pursuing only him." Overwhelmed by fear and running for my life, I cry out to God, "I feel like King Jehoshaphat when the entire Aramean Army was pursuing only him."

"Peace, glorious peace; I can stay here forever," are my spoken thoughts as I relax in prayer and rest in God's Spirit. Soothing is the work of prayer here in this place that has been made into a sanctuary of faith, hope, and love, from which I know what awaits me one step away.

Suddenly, my unguarded sanctuary became chilly, as if someone left an outside door wide open. This is followed by a musty smell entering where it is unwanted. "Be gone," I yell out loud. But my words mean nothing nor accomplish anything regarding what they are sent out to do. They were powerless against the advancing nightmare.

It was then that God's voice broke through to my heart. *My Word will not return to me void, but accomplish what it was sent out to do.*[44]

I know what this means, but I do not want to accept it. For in doing so I will have to move forward from this temporary haven of restful peace. But this I also know: regardless of my attitude, the other side of that open door awaits me.

Trembling at that thought, I become wheezy and sick to my stomach. Gone now are the feelings of peace and restful spirit and confident heart as I replace them with fears that were not meant to be.

I know what I must do, but I resist doing so. How long can I hold out from going through that lousy door? As long as it takes. "Yes," I say, "as long as it takes."

"Robert."

As a child who does not want to hear his parent, I start to raise my hands to cover both ears.

"Robert."

Just another twelve inches, and I can defy. "My God, what am I doing?"

Down to my knees I drop. Down to the ground my head goes. Outstretched before me are my arms. My hands lay flat on the ground far from my ears. With eyes closed and heart open, I brace myself for what I deserve.

FORGIVENESS.
HOW CAN I BE?

Do not remember the sins of my youth, nor my transgressions; According to Your mercy remember me, For Your goodness' sake, O Lord.

Have I gone too far in my rebellious spirit this time? Thoughts and feelings drain out of me like iced tea through an open spigot.

How long can I survive in this state? Not long. Not long at all. Beneath me the ground is damp with my perspiration. By slightly lifting my head, I can barely see the outline of that lousy door ahead of me.

With a long, drawn-out sigh, I drop my head again, clunking it on the path's hard surface.

"What's this?" I ask myself as my mind diverts itself to something new, something strange. The musty smells of this wretched place are starting to give way to ...

"Is this what I think it is?"

"Yes it is, Robert. Breathe it in, and stand up before me."

I ask myself, *How can I stand before Almighty God, Creator of heaven and earth and sustainer of all life? I can-*

not, my heart informs me. My soul overrides that negative advice by bringing Jesus's words to my mind: "Come unto me, all ye that labor and are heavy laden; and I will give you rest."[45]

Rest. If there are perfect words, *rest* must be near the list's top. Pleasant thoughts of rest are cut short as my mind flashes back to Nam, where once again I am pulling twenty-plus-hour days.

We got up prior to dawn to ready ourselves and our Tracks (Dusters) to roll at first light. The rest of the day would be spent escorting infantry or combat engineers farther out into the boonies and then guarding them, always alert, always scanning, always ready to act on impulse at first signs or sounds of danger. If a makeshift fire base or landing zone was not created, we would then escort our brood back from which they came. We then would go on to our small, isolated fire base.

Arriving shortly before sunset, we would refuel and rearm our Tracks, clean our weapons, clean ourselves as much as possible, eat our C-rations, and start pulling two two-hour shifts of guard duty either on our Tracks or in bunkers. We would consider ourselves fortunate if we received two two-hour shifts of sleep per night. If our small firebases received incoming, we Duster crewmembers would have to climb up into our Tracks in less than a minute to return fire and remain alert until all danger was over.

Then, shortly before dawn, we would once again get up to prepare our Tracks and ourselves for another repeat of yesterday. It was easy to lose count of yesterdays unless you kept a personal calendar of countdown days until your trip home from vacation wonderland.

Exhausted from the flashback, I nearly forgot what triggered my blast to the past. What peace I had evaporated like Vietnam's infringing eerie morning mist.

Oh yes. Breathe in deep, and stand up.

Following the first part of the Lord's command, I breathe in the aroma-charged air of hyssop, rose, and spit that fills my heart, soul, and mind with penetrating thoughts of His Word:

> Purge me with hyssop, and I shall be clean: wash me, and I shall be whiter than snow.
>
> Psalm 51:7

> I am the Rose of Sharon, The lily of the valleys.
>
> Song of Solomon 2:1

> When He had thus spoken, He spat on the ground, and made clay of the spittle, and He anointed the eyes of the blind man with the clay.
>
> John 9:6

"Lord, purge me, for I want to be clean before you. Wash me, for I want to be pure before you. Lord, as the roses of Sharon and the lilies of the valleys bring delight to our senses of sight, smell, and touch, so you bring delight into my life in this darkened realm of misery. Lord, help me to see the beauty of your will for my life in this sunken trench of PTSD. Amen."

"Father, Lord God Almighty, I want to stand up before you. This is true. But once I do, I know you will point me to that door like a mother bird pushes her young out of the nest. They fly and in so doing experience newfound freedom. I'll crash and experience more enslavement to PTSD."

"Forgive me, Lord, for looking upon my fears rather than upon your Word that is perfect and altogether lovely."[46]

I'm trembling like a newborn fawn upon its first attempt to stand followed by walking. Knowing what I must do, I look, but He is not there.

"Lord, I cannot see you. Where are you?"

"I'm right here, as I have always been."

"But, Lord—"

"Robert, you do not need to see me. You need to trust me. In that trust, you will find the strength to obey me through faith. Remember, Robert, that I am the author and finisher of your faith."[47]

No longer am I trembling. I'm frozen in place like a deer caught in the headlights of an oncoming vehicle. Who am I that I am so loved by God? I'm so unworthy and undeserving of such love.

My mind goes back in time through a litany of bad behavior, rebellious thoughts and actions, hatreds, and an unending host of sins for which I am ashamed. I have been forgiven of them through salvation in Christ Jesus upon his Father's will.[48] But it's hard to convince my fear-struck heart of this truth until it could take no more.

At this pivoting moment, my heart cries out unto God, *Do not remember the sins of my youth, nor my transgressions; according to your mercy remember me, for your goodness' sake, Oh Lord.*

Forgiveness is another word near the list's top of perfect words. If only I could convince myself to walk through life in this assurance of forgiveness. Not a man-centered assurance, but one from the heavenly throne room of God.[49]

Meditating on the wonderful truths of peace and for-giveness, I find myself rising to stand before the Lord, my Maker, in whom I believe and trust. [50]

────────────────────

Life is filled with too many doors, each door represent-ing an opportunity that will lead me farther from the moment in which I'm dwelling.

He who stands knocking at the doors of human hearts[51] is with me this side and the other side of the door that awaits me. The Lord Jesus Christ has knocked many a time on my heart's door. I'm trying to learn not to keep Him waiting. Sometimes it's a losing battle. Oh, but the times it's not, how glorious and beyond measure are the untold blessings of an open heart to the Word and Spirit of God.

FOR GOODNESS' SAKE, KNOCK! KNOCK!

> Good and upright is the Lord; Therefore He teaches sinners in the way.

This much-needed rest has strengthened my resolve to face that which is yet to come, whatever it may be. To assure this moment isn't merely pleasant feelings but a soul-strengthening reality, I call out, "Good and upright is the Lord: therefore will He teach sinners in the way."

Lowering my head, I continue pleading, "Teach me, Lord, for I am a sinner saved by grace. This sinner needs you to teach me further how to walk as you would have me walk, trust as you would have me trust, believe as you would have me believe."

Taking a deep breath, I slowly raise my head and open my eyes to face that which I dread: the door, that lousy door. I close my eyes, take another deep breath, and step forward.

Closer, still closer I drag myself toward that threatening silhouette until I see it up close. My shuffling feet rebel by digging their heels into the hard, crusted ruts underneath them. My mind tries to override my feet, but my body joins in the mutiny.

There I stand, inches from the portal I must faithfully follow God's Spirit through.

Knock! Knock!

As the Lord knocks at my heart's door, Ernie comes to mind. Ernie is a three-year-old basset retriever, who on occasions digs all four paws in the ground while trying his best to wiggle free from the leash and collar. Low to the ground and sixty pounds of muscle, he's nearly impossible to drag through the front door into the living room if he wants to stay outside.

Knock! Knock!

"I know who's there."

Knock! Knock!

"I know, Lord. I know."

Knock! Knock!

"I'm trying, Lord."

Knock! Knock!

"This portal before me is becoming more menacing the longer I resist."

Knock! Knock!

"What? Can't you see I'm having issues here?"

Knock! Knock!

"Oh. I give up. Here goes nothin.'"

One step forward. "That wasn't too bad." Second step. "It's getting a little easier." Third step. "Wait one minute here! What's this?"

There's enough light, dim as it may be, to see what resembles four deeply worn, narrow grooves about shoulder height in both doorposts.

"That's strange. What could have made those marks?"

Knock! Knock!

"Yes. I know, Lord. I must trust you and obey your Spirit's leading. This I know, for the Bible tells me so."[52]

My mind floats back to early childhood in Southside Chicago during the 1950s. There, in a church basement surrounded by other children all facing forward, looking upon saintly women with smiling faces and sparkling eyes, we learned a fundamental truth put to song:

> Jesus loves me, this I know; for the Bible tells me so. Little ones to him belong; they are weak, but he is strong. Yes, Jesus loves me. Yes, Jesus loves me. Yes, Jesus loves me. The Bible tells me so.[53]

With almost a smile on my face, I step forward to pass through the portal when suddenly PTSD's wretched disparity hits me full force. Instinctively, I reach out my arms to steady myself. In doing so, my fingers slip into the narrow smooth grooves.

As my fingertips begin slipping down the grooves' length, I realize I'm the latest of countless millions before me. Franticly digging my feet into the ground, I strive to stiffen my fingers in hopes of gaining leverage.

As I scream out to God, additional forces hit me from all directions. My lungs feel like deflated balloons as I gasp for air in what seems to be a smoke-filled room.

Knock! Knock!

HUMBLE JUSTICE VERSUS INJUSTICES

The humble He guides in justice, And the humble He teaches His way.

"Lord, what have I done to come under your judgment?"

Like a super-charged computer, my mind rapidly searches for offenses against God in my memory. Then, with lightning speed, sins are flashed before my eyes, causing me to cry out, "I'm doomed."

Now my heart, like a computerized game, unleashes a barrage of injustices against family, friends, and others that I have committed down through the decades.

In deep emotional anguish and agonizing pain, I cry out, "For which of these sins am I being judged?"

No response. There is nothing more terrifying at this point than silence. My mind flashes back to two years of age when I was held hostage by an acute kidney disease. I pivoted dead center on the scales of life and death for months. During that critical time, my parents and grandmother tended me at home the best they could, never wavering in their vigilant faith, hope, and prayers.

Flashing forward, endless scenes of parental sacrificial acts of love cascaded before me in brilliant colors, attaching themselves to my conscience. Unable to disconnect this internal channel to my soul, my mind snatches a recent scene from my past.

"Lord, this has to be the sin you are judging me for because it is shameful unto me."

This must be it because I absolutely do not want to deal with it. Just the thought of revisiting this unresolved episode causes me great anguish, sending chills down my neck, arms, and legs.

As my entire body shivers uncontrollably, my raw fingertips finally surrender in pain. Down I fall to my knees, exhausted, shivering, and numb.

"Arise and stand before me, Robert."

"God, I have no strength left. And I am of no further use to you, myself, or anyone else. Please, Lord, have mercy. I cannot bear the thought of standing before your holiness from which I am about to be judged, condemned, and sentenced."

"Robert, arise and stand before me."

"Lord God Almighty, I never thought it would come to this: condemnation rather than salvation. I'm too tired and numb to ..."

Suddenly I feel a warm, firm hand under my sweaty chin, tenderly lifting it. This is followed by another equally gentle, firm hand upon my lower back, slowly lifting and guiding me to my feet.[54]

I dare not open my eyes, for I know who holds me in the palm of his hand. Ashamed and deeply grieved, I try bowing my head but am unable. I try kneeling but am unable. I try stepping backward but am unable. I try speaking self-incriminating words but am unable.

Gently and tenderly, my quivering body is drawn closer into the bosom of Abraham, the very presence of God Almighty.[55]

Once again, the Prince of Peace brings to light in my life that which fear hindered: peace. As my fears and anxiousness give way to peace, my mind begins to unwind, my heart begins to soften, and my spirit begins to rest.[56]

"Robert, it is time to move on from this place."

Basking in the Lord's peace, I pray, "Oh God, please allow me to stay right here for a little longer. My fingers hurt. My shoulders feel out of joint. My legs feel like bungee cords without elasticity. And my toes are throbbing something fierce."

"These things are of your own making, the fruit of your unbelief and fears."

These words cut to the core, striking fear to my heart: a holy fear activated and unleashed by the truth I wish to deny altogether. I am reaping what I have sown. The length and degree of this reaping is not up to me but to the Lord.[57]

Exhausted yet refreshed, I ponder further on those stinging words. "Here I stand," I tell myself, "and from here I shall step forth in faith, knowing Jesus is with me. I need not fear his judgments, for they are just; and from here, I'll walk forth in his justice."[58]

I believe this. I have to believe this. "God help me believe this."

CHOOSING WISELY.
LEARNING TO CHOOSE

All the paths of the Lord are mercy and truth, To such as keep His covenant and His testimonies.

Shivering myself awake, I'm startled by the dark and dingy surroundings. When my eyes adjust to the shadowy depths, I realize where I am.

"Was it all a dream?" I ask myself.

If it was a dream, it captivated my heart, soul, and mind just as if I lived through every second of it. I have had realistic dreams before, but nothing like this one.

My mind is filled with wonder. My heart is thrilled beyond measure. My body is completely relaxed. I cannot remember such an experience in this sunken trench of PTSD. *It almost makes it bearable,* I tell myself.

Bang! My moment of tranquility bursts like a large balloon. Instinctively, I dive to the ground, covering my head.

"Lord, what happened? I felt so peaceful, just as if I was in your presence."

"You were, Robert. You still are."

"But, Lord, why did you shatter my peace? I don't understand. I'm confused."

"I did not burst your peace of mind and heart.[59] You did that yourself. You sabotaged yourself with your lack of faith and confidence in me.[60]

Rattled to the core, all I can think of or respond with is, "What?"

He then addressed me as one with little faith and asked a piercing question: "Why did you doubt?"[61]

Speechless, my mind locks in on Peter when Jesus granted him permission to step out of a boat to walk toward him on the water. Without hesitation, Peter stepped out onto the water and walked toward Jesus.[62]

My mind goes back to that historical walk when faith overrode buoyancy until sinking Peter yelled, "Lord, save me."

Instantly, Jesus saved Peter from a watery grave, and together they walked to the bobbing boat. During that walk Jesus spoke to him, saying, "O you of little faith, why did you doubt?"

Peter was speechless. I understand why. I never stepped out of a perfectly good boat to walk on water. But I have stepped beyond my comfort zone in hopes of accomplishing some great things only to panic after a few steps.

At times, like Peter, I do not make it very far before the reality of what I'm doing hits me like a ton of fish. At only 195 pounds, I sink into a smelly mess. And, like Peter, I yell to the Lord, who hears my desperate cry and saves me from my undoing.

This whole episode reminds me that walking by faith is walking toward the Lord, who is already where I am hoping to go.[63]

I get it, Lord. I get it. I am to walk by faith, not by sight. Your patience with me is endless, just as is your mercy and kindness. I'm truly grateful for each of these priceless gifts extended to me from your heavenly throne.[64]

Once again my mind reverts back to the Bible, in which Jesus encounters a desperate father seeking help for his son from the disciples. The father grew more desperate as the disciples' inability to bring healing became more evident.[65]

Meditating on that, I think out loud: "Then Jesus came. Then his pointed question and comment came. Then the father's desperate prayer came: 'Lord, I do believe. Help my unbelief.'"

That same frantic plea has since been uttered by countless millions of distressed believers down through the ages. This I know, for I am one of them.

Thinking out loud again, I continue with, "Then Jesus came."

The question he asked Peter he still asks of me: "O you of little faith, why did you doubt?"

The statement he voiced to the desperate father is also being spoken to me: "If you can believe, all things are possible to him who believes."

And my responses remain the same as Peter's speechlessness and the anxious father's: "Lord, I do believe. Help my unbelief."

Exhausted but wiser, I am ready to move on from here in the knowledge of lessons relearned.

Reassuring myself through faith in Christ, I stand up to face that which lies ahead of me and he who awaits me there.

"Breathe," I tell myself. "Breathe in deep and long." The air is stale but breathable as I say, "'All the paths of the Lord are mercy and truth, to such as keep His covenant and His testimonies.' I am such a man, knowing it's not by my might or power but by the Spirit of God."[66]

My loud voice sounds hollow in the long, deep, dark trench into which I stare. Looking down to get my bearings, I notice a welcome sight: footprints, all of which are facing forward.

With half a smile I say, "Lord, they remind me of sheep," to which God immediately places on my mind Isaiah 53:6: "All we like sheep have gone astray; we have turned; every one, to his own way; and the Lord has laid on Him the iniquity of us all."

"Yes, Lord, I acknowledge my sin before you. I am like a lamb gone astray, looking for greener pastures; a wayward lamb by choice, turning from your paths to make my own way. But the outcome always remains the same: artificial turf.

PARDON MY INIQUITY PLEASE

> For Your name's sake, O Lord, Pardon my iniq-
> uity, for it is great.

Facing that which I dread and loathe, I take one more
deep breath, followed by my first step forward and then
straight down to my knees. On my knees, I continue
looking into the colorless, miserable face of PTSD as I
raise my hands to the Lord in prayer. From the depths of
my soul flows forth a prayer: *For your name's sake, oh Lord,
pardon my iniquity, for it is great.*

Kneeling in this trench worn into the bottom of the
valley of the shadow of death, I thank God for hearing
and answering my prayer.

Still kneeling, I take another deep breath. Beginning
to stand, I am catapulted into what had to be a dream,
during which all sense of time is lost.

"Where am I?"

"You are in contempt of court."

"What?"

"A 'watt,' you say? Do I look like a light bulb to you? You remain silent before me in this my court. Do you understand?"

"No, I do not."

"You do not what?"

"I do not understand any of this. I do not know how I got here. I don't even know where or what 'here' is. And I've never laid eyes on you before."

"Before this hearing is up, you will wish I never existed, especially after this court finishes with you."

"But—"

"Silence yourself. You will speak only when spoken to. I remind you, for the last time, you are in my court. There will be no more outbursts by the likes of you."

"You can't be serious. This is all a mistake."

Bang, goes the gavel on the worn oak block. The resulting sound rings throughout the courtroom, nearly piercing my eardrums.

"You are in contempt. This court fines you five hundred dollars and sentences you to five days of hard labor."

"What?"

"Make that a thousand dollars and ten days of hard labor."

"This is a sham. You have no authority over me. You might as well fine me a million dollars and throw me in prison forever because you are nothing to me; nothing at all, I tell you. Nothing but a bad, awful nightmare."

The judge instantly jumps to his feet, yelling at the top of his lungs into a lapel microphone, "So let it be." Just as quickly, he bends down to grab something on the floor, from which he raises a sledgehammer up over and behind his head. With a full swing he brings down that hammer on the solid oak block, splitting it in two.

"Guilty, guilty, guilty. You are guilty of trespassing on government property with intent of bringing down our strongholds."[67]

With that, the jury jumps to its feet, singing, "Guilty, guilty, guilty. You are guilty of trespassing against our government and against us its citizens." They sing it repeatedly, raising their voices and pitch after each frame.

In the middle of this insanity, six tall, muscular, heavily armed guards burst into the courtroom from the judge's chambers. Drawing their pistols, they encircle me, watching my every motion.

"Take him, boys," the judge says in a deep, menacing voice.

Before the words are out of his mouth, the guards jump me with all their might. Crushed beneath their weight, I am defenseless against their assault. Standing me upright, they bind and gag me, placing a large dog collar around my neck. Each guard then attaches a thick chain to my collar. The weight nearly takes me to my knees.

In total disbelief, I try to cry out but cannot because of the collar digging into my neck. My ears hurt from the raging noise of the chaotic courtroom. My neck is about to snap. Barely breathing, I faint. Pulling on their chains, the guards raise me up by the dog collar around my neck.

Drifting in and out of consciousness, I try to convince myself this whole thing is nothing more than a bad nightmare. Suddenly, I'm jolted back into consciousness by the judge's voice.

"Boy, this is no dream. You are in my court. That's for sure."

With that, he commands the guards to take all my belongings and identification. After doing so, they are commanded to remove me from his sight and throw me into the deepest dungeon within the walled prison.

"It's time to wake up, Bob. Wake up before it's too late. Wake up. I have to get myself to wake up."

The judge laughingly yells, "Too late. It is too late for you."

At that, the whole courtroom erupts into a thunderous chorus of, "It's too late for you. Ha ha ha. It's too late for you. Ha ha ha."

The guards take me through the door, slamming it behind them. All goes dark and silent. For how long I do not know.

From somewhere within this silence I hear a firm, commanding voice say, "Securely bind those renegade guards with their own chains, making escape impossible. Then cast them one by one into our deepest fiery dungeon that awaits the likes of them and their master."

From somewhere I hear six separate terrible screams of terror. Each of these is followed by noxious odors of sulfur and brimstone, as if a door was opened and shut six times.

Then a gentle voice of mercy speaks my name. "Robert."

"Yes, Lord. I am listening."

"You are safe. You were always safe, even in that illegitimate courtroom. Never were you out of my sight. Nor will you ever be. Do you believe this?"[68]

"Yes, my Lord, I believe you."

"Why do you believe me?"

"Oh Lord my God, your name is holy,[69] as is your kingdom. I was born into sin, but you took me in.[70] While still your enemy, you reconciled me unto yourself,[71] after which you entrusted the ministry of reconciliation unto me[72] and commissioned me to forgive as you have forgiven me[73] and to love as you have loved me."[74]

"Yes, I did. And you?"

"Lord, I confess to you there are times I'm doubtful like Gideon,[75] find fault with myself like Moses,[76] and grumble like the sons of Israel.[77] I act too big for my britches like Samson,[78] I stumble like King David,[79] I'm impatient like Sarah,[80] and I feel insignificant like Zaccheus.[81] I'm too busy to catch the significance of the moment like Martha[82] or stick my foot in my mouth like Peter.[83] And, Lord, just as you turned all those faults into blessings, you do so in my life."[84]

With that, I am back on my knees, looking into the colorless, miserable face of PTSD.

HOLY FEAR VERSUS OH DEAR

Who is the man who fears the Lord? Him shall
He teach in the way He chooses.

"Was it all a dream?" I ask myself.

Thinking out loud, I continue. "If it was a dream, it captivated my heart, soul, and mind, just as if I lived through every second of it. I have had realistic dreams before, but nothing like this one. My goodness, how many of these have I had?"

Reflecting out loud, I ask, "How many more can I handle?"

That gets me to wondering about my whole Vietnam experience. There have been times through decades past when my tour of duty in Vietnam resembled a dream more than a reality. Yet I have more vivid memories of my tour of duty than any other year of my life.

Those ten months are the seedbed into which nightmares and flashbacks have established their diabolical roots. Once established, roots are quickly sent deep into the rich soil of misery that is fertilized regularly with pain and sorrow.

Lowering my eyes, I can see the trench's hardened floor illuminated right in front of my knees. This inspires me to quote the comforting truth of Psalm 119:105: "Your word is a lamp to my feet And a light to my path."

"Even down here your Word is a lamp unto my feet, and a much-needed light on this path I have been traveling. For this I am very grateful. Without it, I would aimlessly wander around in my fears and anger."[85]

The words of my prayer leap into my mind, causing me to think what it would be like dwelling in this despicable place without hope. Instantly overcome by the willies, I fiercely wag my head to jar loose such a terrible thought.

"Oh Lord, this sunken path I dwell and walk in is terrible to all my senses, yet I have you as the hope of my life.[86] You know my heart.[87] You know I love you, but I hate this place. Actually, I loathe it with every fiber of my body. But you I trust. Help me to trust you more, a whole lot more."

Knowing it is time to move on from here, I prepare myself by submitting my heart to worship the Lord. If I do not submit my heart, it will be the first source of rebellion in my life against God and his kingdom.[88]

> To You, O Lord, I lift up my soul. O my God, I trust in You; let me not be ashamed; let not my enemies triumph over me. Indeed, let no one who waits on You be ashamed; let those be ashamed who deal treacherously without cause. Show me Your ways, O Lord; teach me Your paths. Lead me in Your truth and teach me, for You are the God of my salvation; on You do I wait all the day. Remember, O Lord, Your tender mercies and Your lovingkindnesses, for they are from of old.

Do not remember the sins of my youth, nor my transgressions; according to Your mercy remember me, for Your goodness' sake, O Lord. Good and upright is the Lord; therefore He teaches sinners in the way. The humble He guides in justice, and the humble He teaches His way. All the paths of the Lord are mercy and truth, to such as keep His covenant and His testimonies. For Your name's sake, O Lord, pardon my iniquity, for it is great. Who is the man who fears the Lord? Him shall He teach in the way He chooses.

Psalm 25:1–12

"O Lord God Almighty, Creator and sustainer of life, to you I submit my life, worshiping you in holy fear and reverence. I kneel here in awe of you: my Creator and Redeemer. Your love for me never lost its grip of my soul, even when I was caught up in the bloodshed of war.[89] Your pure love held me extra tight as I left the battlefields of Vietnam for my re-entry into America, only to be declared an enemy by some fellow Americans. You have never lost sight or hold of my life when I fell prey to PTSD, totally unaware of its infiltration until the results of its mutilations started wreaking havoc in everything I held dear."

Standing up, I stretch and then take in a deep breath to continue praying. "I know my life is in your hands and acknowledge there is no safer place for it.[90] Forgive me for the times I fret about how I would do things differently and for those times I actually do so. Help me to take my medicine when I trespass against your will for my life. Reaping what I sow is humbling and at times hard to take, but I'm a better man afterward. Thank you for never giving up on me as you teach me how to live and walk in the way you personally have chosen for me bet foundations of the world."[91]

Facing the cold, darkened trench before me, I finis my prayer. "Dear Father, who else do I have in heaven but you?[92] The thought of your throne and throne room thrill me and give me hope. Help me now, I pray thee, to face this ongoing journey with confidence in Christ Jesus, my living hope, who promises never to leave me or forsake me."[93]

With another deep breath, followed by a hearty "amen," I step forth on the path set before me in the trench of PTSD cut into the bottom of the valley of the shadow of death.

HOPE FOR THOSE BRUTALIZED BY PTSD

He himself shall dwell in prosperity, And his descendents shall inherit the earth.

"Whistle while you walk...I'll be coming up the trench when I come...Three blind mice...Three blind preachers...Three blind steps; see how I stumble, see how I get up, see how I keep going...Jesus loves all the children, all the children in this trench...Jesus loves me this I know, for he told me so, before throwing me in this place."

Stopping in midstep, I stop singing and start praying, "God, I'm sorry for singing that. You didn't throw me in here on my face and stomp me into submission. I don't even want to go there, for nothing is further from the truth. For me, this trench of PTSD in which I exist is the result of my time fighting in Vietnam, not the result of offending an angry God. Please forgive me. I am without excuse. I am in your hands."

Silence overcomes my spoken prayer just like a thick pillow silences a ticking clock. Standing in this stillness, I start advising myself, "Scholten," then breaking into song. "You better wise up, for one of the wise men you're not."

Standing alone in my thoughts, I begin wondering how long I've been shuffling along in this life-zapping existence that imitates normalcy but fails miserably. One easily loses sense of time in a life of PTSD. What day is it, anyway? At one time a long time ago I didn't have to think twice, because the moment of the hour of the day of the week of the month of the year of the decade was instantaneously present at all times.

Thinking back to a time in which I lived a normal life, a stark reality hits me for the first time: I only had twenty years of normalcy before Vietnam ripped it out of my life. "But what a life it has been." I had been constantly on the move as if running from something to something else or from somewhere to somewhere else.

Continuing in thought, my family comes to mind and with them, a smile to my face and heart.

"Thank God Cheryl never had a clue what she was saying 'I do' to. Come to think of it, neither did I at that time. I just thought my altered life was a normal one. How wrong I was."

Laughing, and then laughing some more, I yell until it echoes back again and again, "God has taken that which was meant for evil and turned it into a blessing, a rich blessing at that. Thank you, Lord. Thank you so very much."

Meditating in deep thought, I speak truth to my heart: "My family has never left me, but I sure have left them more times than I want to admit. I have never physically left those I love and cherish. Emotional and mental abandonment is another matter, a sad reality on my part until this day. God, have mercy on me and especially on my daughters and wife, on my congregation, relatives, friends, and fellow sojourners in PTSD."

Continuing in thought, I momentarily let my guard down. Within a flash, a well-guarded hardship slips from a locked chamber deep in my heart into the forefront of my mind. Caught off guard, I try unsuccessfully to return this difficulty back from which it came.

All my attempts are futile. So many are they that I am about to break down my defenses and neutralize my booby traps. But with one more major offensive to block all thoughts and feelings pertaining to this hardship, along with casting myself into a state of denial, I finally manage to stuff them all back down.

Annoyed, frustrated, and completely worn out, I slump into a fetal position, gasping for air while pushing back tears. Tears. I have only cried once since Vietnam. Tears of laughter, tears of joy, tears of sorrow, and tears of mourning are nonexistent in my life. "Someday I might be blessed with some," I think out loud, surprising myself with such words.

Sitting here, my family comes near, yet they are far. It is hard to explain. It's a reality known by those of us here in this trench in the bottom of the valley of the shadow of death. It also causes confusion in my precious family's life. "Oh God, have mercy and restore the joy of your salvation unto me before I drag my loved ones down into this pit."[94]

Occasionally I do pull my family down here with me, which terrorizes them, filling their hearts with fear, so I release them with a prayer. Then, from there, we work at our frazzled relationship from two different perspectives united by Christ Jesus into one—I, coming to the table of healing from the depths of PTSD, and my family coming to this same table from the heights above the valley of the shadow of death.

We come to this table of healing set by Jesus our Lord and monitored by the Holy Spirit, our perfect comforter and counselor. Here at this table, we as a family listen to our counselor and respond to his counsel. We listen some more, and at his bidding, we listen intently to each other, confessing our hurts and fears, our doubts and concerns.[95] Through it all, we embrace each other while the Master of the table embraces us with his healing touch.

With our hope renewed, love strengthened, minds refreshed, and hearts mended, we bless the Lord and join with his Spirit in giving thanks to our heavenly Father, who made all this possible in and from his heart.

We stand up and walk from the table together as a family. We press forward together in prayer and faith. My family travels the high road above the valley of the shadow of death while I the low road of PTSD etched in the bottom of that valley.

We continually pray for each other as we hold firm these eternal truths that unite and empower us: God is sovereign,[96] his Word is absolute,[97] his saving power through Jesus is eternal,[98] and his grace is gracious indeed.[99]

We, as a family, share these simple yet profound words with all who listen: "We are a family, a family brutalized by Post Traumatic Stress Disorder. We are a family of hope by means of God's Word and sovereignty over us."

Once again stepping off on another segment of this endless journey, I do so, meditating on, "I will dwell in the goodness of God, and my children and their children's children will inherit the earth. And they shall serve the Lord our God who calls them unto himself, not because of who they are but because of who he is."[100]

"Wow, what a day! Or has it been a week or a month or a year? I sure do lose all sense of time down here in this trench. But that is okay because I know who is waiting for me. And glorious will be that day."[101]

Shuffling forward with a song in my heart, I sing it aloud, listening to my echoing choir that accompanies me. "Jesus loves me, this I know, for the Bible tells me so. I am weak, but he is strong. With me he travels along. Yes, Jesus loves me. Yes, Jesus loves me."

A SECRET WELL
WORTH KNOWING

The secret of the Lord is with those who fear
Him, And He will show them His covenant.

There are times when I let myself think fondly of people past. This is such a time. I am tired, so very tired
and weary. Weary of...My lamenting is cut short by the
sword of the Spirit[102] that slices off a chunk of self-pity.

The Word of God never misses what it is meant to
accomplish in the hand of the master swordsman, Jesus
Christ himself.[103] My mind and heart react in unison by
creating a prayer that I lift with bowed head to the Lord.

"I don't have a chance against your accurate swipes
and stabs into my life with the Bible. You are flawless
in your swordsmanship, hitting the mark every time. To
you, Lord, I yield myself as a conquered soul of your gracious right hand [104] over and in my life."

Lifting my head, I see something totally unexpected.
There, coming out of the darkness, is a host of individuals walking straight toward me.

In disbelief, I tightly close my eyes while shaking my head back and forth. Then, after rubbing my closed eyelids with my knuckles, I open them to see if what I saw was real.

"There they are," I say out loud. "They really are walking toward me."

For the first time, as far as I can remember, I throw off caution and run forward to meet them. In between breaths I yell out, "Closer. I'm getting closer. I'm coming. Oof." Down I go, skinning my chin, elbows, and knees.

Getting up as fast as possible, I limp toward them, raising my right hand and saying, "I'm okay. I'm okay."

Finally coming to an abrupt halt, I lower my shoulders to slightly bend forward. There, nearly in front of the welcomed crowd, I bend over in pain, placing one hand on the back of my neck and the other on my stomach.

Catching my breath and pushing back the pain, I continue toward the oncoming crowd, never taking my eyes off them. Stubbing my foot on something embedded in the path, I fall headlong on my face again.

Moaning out of pain and embarrassment, I try getting up but fall back down. Rolling over on my back, using my elbows to raise myself to a sitting position, I humble myself before God. Then I pray, "Forgive my foolish behavior of taking my eyes off the path lit by your Word. Please help me not to forget this lesson I have learned so painfully today."

Slowly lifting my head sheepishly like a dog failing to please its master, I look out upon this massive assembly of humanity. I keep watching as they stop just beyond where the shadowy gray colors give way to the darkness of the trench.

Looking at each other, they silently form themselves into columns of twelve, lining up horizontally before me and stretching back into the darkness from which they came. Without a word, the first column looks directly into my eyes and moves forward, stopping just a few feet in front of me.

That's when I notice these are real people, just not flesh and blood. Looking at them in disbelief on the verge of disgust, I hear the Lord's voice speak to my heart, saying, "Do not look on this blessing in disgust or fear, but simply accept from them what they have been assembled here to give you."

With that, the first person on the left steps forward into the light and stops and looks down with twinkling eyes into my eyes. She then smiles the most beautiful smile I have ever seen. I can't take my eyes off the twinkling eyes looking into my eyes as if they were gazing into my soul. Tingling all over, I remember who this is: a Sunday school teacher from my early childhood who patiently and lovingly taught me my first song, "Jesus Loves Me." With one more beautiful smile that melts my fears away, she vanishes.

Then standing there before me is the next person, who, like the first, with twinkling eyes looks down into mine and smiles the most beautiful smile. As my heart starts to melt a little more, he reminds me of an elder who, week after week, sat next to me in church when my father was absent from us, being hospitalized in the Chicago VA hospital. No one knew how afraid I was as a little child of falling off the end of the pew onto the floor.

"No one knew my pain," I said out loud. "No one but the Lord."

With squinty eyes I gaze intently up into the eyes of him who is looking down into mine.

With a lump in my throat, I say, "You're him. You are the one who sat next to me, expelling my fears and comforting my heart."

With a twinkle in his eyes and an ever-growing smile, he too vanishes before me.

Then standing there before me is the next person, who, like the first two, looks down with twinkling eyes into mine and smiles a most beautiful smile. This goes on twelve times. That's when the second rank of twelve individuals steps forward with a child on the far left stepping forward to look deep into my eyes and smile the most beautiful smile. On and on this goes, for how long I do not know.

"Was it moments, hours, or days?" I ask, looking toward the darkened path that stretches into the future. "Wow. I remembered them all, even their names."

That gets me thinking about the sad fact that from first stepping into Vietnam until this event, I couldn't remember names, even the names of people I knew and associated with. In Nam we always went by nicknames. That way we never got to close to each other. The less we knew of each other the better. All we wanted to know was if we could depend on each other. That was all that really mattered. At least that's what we thought at the time.

My thoughts are interrupted by the voice of the Lord: "Robert, my servant and adopted son, did you like my surprise I kept secret until just the right time?"

"Oh Lord my God, I loved it, absolutely loved it beyond measure. Thank you so very much."

"Remember to remember, Robert. All these people in times past did not enter your life haphazardly, but by my perfect council.[105] My promises in my Word are absolute, every single one of them."

"How many, Lord, and for how long did this blessing unfold before me?"

"That is not for you to know but to enjoy and take with you as you continue continuing in my will for your life.[106] Now arise and step forward in the light of the lamp of my Word."

I do just that, taking with me the memories God opened up in my being that only he could do.

ENTANGLEMENT.
THERE IS HELP

My eyes are ever toward the Lord, For He shall pluck my feet out of the net.

Trust is a key factor of mine that often gets in the way. *Wow, where did that come from?* I ask myself, looking around to see if anyone heard me and thus could ask of me, "From where came what?" What would I say?

That thought stops me dead in my tracks. After scratching my head in hopes of coming up with an answer, I find something suitable to sit on, sitting down and moving my bottom around, finally finding the best-cushioned area.

"Ground attack. They're in the wire." I suddenly scream, "Ground attack! They're in the wire." I startle myself awake from a nightmare, still yelling "Where are you guys? Get out here. They're getting through the wire. God, don't let this be the day I die."

After wildly thrashing around on the ground, I man-age to get myself up on my feet. Bent over and gasping for air while standing there in my fears, I calm down enough to realize what just happened. Looking down at my feet and catching my breath enough to speak, I do so to anyone who'd listen. "It was only a dream, a bad one at that. You need not be afraid."

Slowly straightening myself up and carefully stretching, I wipe my sweaty hands in my hair and down the back of my neck. Then, slowly turning in a circular motion, I scan my self-imposed perimeter. After being convinced I am safe for the moment, I cautiously relax enough to allow myself to think. *Memories are a wonderful blessing or a terrifying entanglement within hidden nets that spring up, entrapping me much like a cunning spider's perfectly spun web. A spider that has learned patience pays high dividends in scrumptious meals for the taking.*

I've been a tasty meal to many a nightmare and flashbacks in these decades following Vietnam, in some cases because of self-entanglement, by placing myself in situations I knew best not to.

Calmer but still highly alert, I start looking for what triggered my nightmare.

Speaking to myself, I say, "This one really got me by surprise. I've been doing pretty well at keeping them at bay. I've got to find out what did this to me."

"What are you looking for?"

"Whoa. Where did you come from?"

"I've been here the whole time plus some. Are you going to tell me what you're looking for?"

"I can't believe you've been here this whole time."

"Look, fellow. You called out for anyone listening not to be afraid. Well, I'm not. So what's up, guy? And by the way, why are you here, anyway? You've got to be out of your mind to be here for any length of time."

"I can't agree with you more, my friend." Extending my hand to this stranger—a welcomed stranger at that—I say, "My name's Bob. I've been traveling in this trench for ever so long. I thought I dealt with my Nam issues a long time ago. Man was I wrong."

"Dead wrong, huh?" he stated, extending his hand to me.

"You got that right," I say half laughingly and half seriously. Taking his hand into mine, I continue. "It sure is good to know there is someone else who understands."

"No, Bob. Not just me, Johnny Boy, but many veterans are here as well. Some were here when I arrived, and some have come since. Hey, come to think about it, you should stick around to attend our meetings. You know what I am talking about? It's a support group for us with PTSD."

"Thank you. But I'm not sticking around these parts long."

He tried encouraging me to change my mind. I didn't because I wouldn't.

"Johnny Boy, I'll stick around long enough to find what I was sitting on. It might just be the thing that triggered my nightmare."

"It is what triggered your nightmare. It has set off many a nightmare for many a person. And it's right over there to our left."

Slowly walking over to the object, I keep thinking about the support group. But the more I think on it, the more antsy I become. I whisper to myself, "I've got to stop this. It's making me upset."

"Here it is, Bob," Johnny Boy said to me as he pointed to an old, scuffed-up steamboat trunk.

"Why, it's nothing but a beat-up old trunk of some kind," I say, standing there trying to figure out why this dilapidated piece of junk would trigger so many nightmares and flashbacks.

Bending down before it, I run my hands around the lid's sides. In doing so, I discover two latches without locks under layers of mossy-type stuff.

Upon further examination of the trunk I say, "Let's open it," to which there is no reply.

Opening the left latch, the right one falls off, allowing the heavy lid to snap open and fly up with such force it shakes loose the trunk's corners. The trunk's four sides hit the bottom of the trench so hard that it sounds like four rifle shots. We both hit the ground together, bumping our heads in the process. Rolling over onto our backs, we sit up, rubbing our heads.

Standing up in what seems to be a dust storm, we wave our arms, trying to clear the air so we can see. Sometime later, as the heavy dust particles settle to the ground, we both look at each other in amazement. There in front of us were large, hill-like mounds, way more than the trunk could ever hold.

Reaching over, Johnny Boy sticks his hands in the mound directly in front of us and says, "It's nothing but dirt."

I walk over to the other mound, sticking my right hand into it. After feeling the stuff in my hands and watching it slip down through my fingers, I say, "This isn't dirt. It's sand."

"Hey, Bob. This mound over here is mud."

"That's nothing, Johnny Boy. This one here is sharp, gritty, sandlike stuff."

"I got that beat. This mound I'm standing on is rock. And that one over there looks like mush of some sort. Good grief, Bob. How many of these things are there?"

"Beats me, Johnny Boy. But I think I know what all this is. Let's walk around the perimeter of these things and meet in the middle. You go left, and I'll head out to the right."

We both take off, disappearing into the trench's broad darkness. Slowly walking, I occasionally call out Johnny Boy's name but hear no reply. After what seems like hours, I see the figure of my friend breaking free of the darkness and walking toward me.

"Okay, Bob. What is all this stuff? And I mean all this stuff, every bit of it."

"Don't laugh now, but I think that trunk was some sort of storehouse for ground from battlefields throughout the world that troops would bring home for memorials of remembrance. I didn't purposely bring any of Nam's dirt back with me. But I did find that red mud caked on my jungle boots. I don't remember what happened to it."

"I do, buddy. It's back about twenty mounds that way. You cannot miss it. It is a ten-foot mound of that red stuff they called dirt. It gave me the willies just walking by it."

"Have fun putting all this back into the little trunk. After you fix it, that is."

"No way, Bob. There has to be at least ten acres of that memorial ground stuff. Hey there, friend. Where do you think you're going? I want to introduce you to all the other folks who meet regularly to deal with their PTSD."

"Thanks, but no thanks. No offense, but I have had enough of this place. Give your friends my best. Maybe we will meet up somewhere later on."

We shake hands and give each other a hearty bear hug. No words said, just the nodding of our heads in a farewell gesture.

Regaining my bearings, I slowly walk forward, never looking back. Ever since 1970, when I walked away from my mother and sisters and friends in O'Hare Airport to board that plane, I have never looked back.

After walking what seemed to be a short distance, I stopped and for the first time in decades, began slowly turning around. "What am I doing?" I say with a loud, agitated voice, turning myself frontward again.

From behind me I hear muffled voices saying, "You are coming back here to deal with your unresolved PTSD issues."

"No, I'm not," I answer as I start walking forward again.

And from behind me I could barely hear their response to me: "What are you afraid of?"

Refusing to answer, I shuffle forward but come to an abrupt stop, thinking out loud, "I wonder if Johnny Boy and his friends were God's way of plucking me out of another net." Pausing further in thought, I eventually whisper, "Should've stayed with them for a while."

LONELINESS: AN EVER-PRESENT BATTLE

Turn Yourself to me, and have mercy on me, for I
am desolate and afflicted.

It's amazing what one thinks about while traversing
through life this side of war. I have said it once, and I'll
say it many more times to as many people who will listen:
"War is likened unto salvation. Once you experience it,
your life is never the same." That thought hit me back in
the 1980s, and it hasn't changed since. It cannot change
because war changes people, be they individuals or families
or communities or nations.

"Oh Lord my God, I have so much to learn, even
more to experience, and still more to pray about."

With that prayer, I stop for a much-needed rest. In
doing so, my mind drifts back in time, bringing up from
the depths of my soul faces of those who nurtured me
into a prayer warrior, one who cherishes prayer for what
it is: a way of life for the rest of my life with my Creator
and King; one who, like King David, stumbles and falls
at times but gets up again to continue going forth in the
Lord, rejoicing in his forgiveness and mercy.

Moments later, thinking out loud, I say, "War has not changed that but enhanced it multiple times. I would never tell anyone that fighting in a war is the best way to learn the power and importance of prayer in one's life."

Standing up to leave my restful spot, I sit right back down, nursing another thought, a strange one at that, a three-word phrase: "War and prayer."

"What a thought," I say to myself while shaking my head, followed by scratching the back of my neck with my right hand.

Just sitting there like a bump on a log, I slump forward, catching my chin with my left hand while still scratching my neck with the other hand. "War and prayer," or is it, "Prayer and war?" Let's see here, should it be "praying while in war or at war?"

"Robert."

I jump nearly out of my chair sitting at the head of the dinner table. "Yes, Cheryl? What now?"

"Stop scratching you neck, and eat your food before it gets cold." Lowering her fork into the empty plate in front of her, she asks me, "What were you thinking?"

"Huh?"

"What were you thinking about?"

Saying nothing, I look down at my dinner plate that is nearly full and getting cooler by the minute. Looking back up at Cheryl, I dare not say what was going through my mind, eventually to end up in my heart.

So I sit here, looking at her through eyes that once again start reverting back to Vietnam. Then, once there, they automatically focus into the thousand-yard stare.

I was gone again while still sitting at the dinner table with my family, my precious family, who already are bearing a burden no family should: a husband and a father fallen prey to PTSD.

"Turn yourself to me and have mercy on me, for I am desolate and afflicted," is what I was whispering as I shook myself awake. Moments later I started to think of King David, who, in his loneliness, reached out to God in prayer.

Loneliness is something most war veterans, if not all, know all too well. I'm one of them, which saddens me to admit.

"Turn yourself to me, and have mercy on me, for I am desolate and afflicted." I continue to think, *This must have been etched into David's inner door leading into his heart.*

"'Desolate and afflicted.' Hey, David, general sir, mighty warrior, and Royal Highness, you knew what you were writing about." Lowering my voice to express further thoughts, I speak into the darkness, "Desolation and affliction accurately describe the bitter fruits of warfare."

My deepened thinking is distracting me enough, so I start tripping but steady myself each time. Remembering back to my previous falls, I stop to think things through. To my displeasure, it works all too well by producing something I want to instantly forget but cannot. Affliction is the ever-present sentinel standing guard over my imprisonment in the deep dungeon of loneliness.

"Let me out," I cry aloud, startling myself awake in my bed, in my bedroom, in the manse of the church in which I serve as pastor. "Not again?" Getting out of bed soaking wet from perspiration, I try to calm down.

Instinctively, I turn to prayer and the Bible. Countless times since the age of sixteen, my fingers have flipped through these worn pages of Scriptures to Psalm 25. Once there, my eyes take over to fill my soul with the light of God's Holy Word. Being saturated with biblical truths, my soul then unleashes them through my entire being.

Thus, the timeless power of God's Word passes effortlessly through the heavily guarded door of my heart, where it cleans house. It starts by using the eternal cleanser, which is the eternal truths found in the twenty-fifth Psalm.

Turn to me.

In my loneliness I yearn for someone who understands, but the thought of letting a person that close is out of the question. Therein lays the ever-present sin of distrust with its guardian: fear.

Turn yourself to me, and have mercy on me. Mercy triumphs over judgment;[107] therefore, I cannot survive without it.

TROUBLED HEART: COMING UP OUT OF DISTRESS

> The troubles of my heart have enlarged; bring me
> out of my distresses!

"Ouch!" Backing up from whatever I walked into, I fall backward over something. Lying motionless on the ground, I frantically try regaining my breath. Finally doing so, I manage to groan, "Double ouch! Oh, that hurts. Make it a triple ouch!"

Somewhat delirious from the fall, I start talking to Johnny Boy.

"For days now, Johnny Boy, I have been zigzagging through some nasty places. As you already know, none of them have names. And of course there's never a resting place. You know, Johnny Boy, a real rest stop, for goodness' sake."

"You just lay here, Bob. I'll go get help."

"Okay. Do whatever you have to do."

"It's going to take a while, so don't go wandering off somewhere."

"Yeah, right."

"Here. Let me move you so you'll be more comfortable."

"This ought to be good, a hallucinated Johnny Boy moving a real me. That's funny. Man, you're losing it, Scholten. You're really losing it!"

"Losing what, Bob?"

"I'm losing my mind. What do you think I'm losing?"

"No, Bob. You are not losing your mind. You are of sound mind in a bruised-up body. The fact that you came back to face your fears proves there's something up there in your head and down there in your heart. Here now. One more short lift, and I'll have you in a more comfortable position."

"Oh man. That hurts. Can't you be more gentle? Oh, no. No, no, no! This can't be happening. Tell me it's not so. Is that you, Johnny Boy?"

"It sure is, Bob. You had me worried there for a spell, my friend. I sure am glad you came back. I'm happy you came back to face your fears."

"But—"

"But nothing, Bob. You are back, and that's all that matters. You are back."

"But—"

"Like I said, it's good to see you came back. Now, do not move around much. I'm going to get some of the guys to help get you back, back where you belong."

"But—"

"That's okay. I'm glad to see you too, Bob."

Drifting back to sleep, I dream of yesteryear before PTSD hijacked my life and shanghaied my family. It was a sweet dream.

Rolling over to my side, I get up. At least I try to. Shifting my weight, trying to find a spot that doesn't hurt, I find myself thinking of Uncle Rule. With him on my mind, I drift back to sleep dreaming of my great-uncle who did a great deed.

Drifting gently, drifting softly, drifting slowly, all was well in my life, in my mother's arms, in a small boat, in a large lake, in Wisconsin, in the year of 1950 when I was but an infant, an infant snuggled safely in a loving mother's arms, in a gently drifting boat with three adults who loved me beyond measure.

"That kid in that speedboat is getting pretty close," said Great Uncle Rule. "He is getting too—"

"Where's my baby? Where's my baby?" a frantic mother screams as she tries to keep herself above water.

"I see him, Grace. I see Bobby," my Great-Uncle Rule cries out as he swims toward little circular ripples drifting outward on the water's surface. Swimming and praying, he reaches me on my third bob.

The whole time this was happening, my father had me in the palm of his hand as he swam upward from the depths of the lake. Swimming with one arm extended as far above his head as possible, he'd get my head slightly above the water's surface before slipping back down into the depths.

"Bertus was discharged from the army after having majority of his stomach removed, thus his energy level would drop quickly."

It was on the third bob that my Great Uncle Rule reached the circling ripples, grabbing me from my father's hand, first placing me securely in the crook of his left arm and then reaching down into the water with his right hand, grabbing hold of my father's hair, during all this keeping afloat by treading water with his legs and feet.

As he is holding me, treading water, praying, and bringing up my father's body, another boat arrives. Its drunken occupant, with God's mercy, helps get me, my mom, my dad's body, and finally my Great Uncle Rule into the safety of his boat.

Moments later, relatives and strangers encircle my family on shore's edge, looking down upon us in disbelief. From out of this shocked group of people a person steps forward. Bending down over my father's lifeless body, this stranger begins resuscitating him under the tearful eyes of a family circle on the verge of being broken.

Surrounded by and lifted up in prayers, my father sits up to the applause of his family not broken and that of heaven above.

I awake to the sound of applauding hands only to discover they are mine. Sitting up, I rub my hands across my flannel shirt to wipe off the water.

"What's this? I'm not wet."

Standing up to stretch, I pause to think. *I'm not wet because that was a dream.* Bewildered, I look downward at what I just rose upward from, thinking out loud while scratching the back of my neck, saying, "Isn't my body supposed to be hurting really bad? Don't tell me that was a dream too? Wait a minute. Do tell me it was a dream. Man am I glad Johnny Boy was nothing but a dream."

I start walking forward, happy at not being wet or all bruised up when, suddenly, I'm down on my face again.

"Now what did I trip over?" Getting up on my feet to look back down, I see what tripped me. "Twice now you tripped me," I yell at the log while kicking it.

Not satisfied with my assault against this good-for-nothing log, I yell at it. Then, winding myself up like a major league baseball pitcher, I let loose with a log-splitting kick.

Coming to again, I get up, rubbing the back of my hurting head. "How could I miss that lousy, good-for-nothing chunk of wood disguised as a log?"

Turning around to see what I smacked my head on, I couldn't believe my eyes. There in front of me was something that resembled the Vietnam memorial.

Motionless and speechless, I just stand there, looking at this tall, wide, black monument. Looking ever so long, I lose myself in thoughts that slip into past memories and then move forward to more recent ones. Finally, after shaking my head and rubbing my eyes, I push back the tears before any drop free—all those tears working their way up to my eyes, seeking their escape from my imprisonment of them forty years earlier.

Growing numb, I slowly shuffle my feet backward until the heels of my shoes touch that log. Bending my knees, I lower myself to a sitting position on that good old log, never taking my eyes off the wall.

For how long I sat I do not know. Neither do I know how much longer I would sit. Years and years of memories were beginning to surface.

"Stop right there!" I yell. "That's far enough. Stop, I say."

As the most recent memories were subsiding, they opened the way for deeper memories to rise up closer into this very moment I was wrestling with. Wanting to stand up, I placed my hands on the moss-covered log only to have them slip off, taking me with them to the ground.

On my hands and knees, I rock myself backward back onto the log. With the wall in front of me and the log beneath me, I shut my eyes as tightly as possible. There, becoming a human bump on a log that had more sense than me, I welcomed the numbness that was returning to its rightful place.

Dropping fast—one, two, three—it won't affect me. Grieve. I cannot do. I must not do. I won't do. I am tearless in the valley of the shadow of death and emotionless in the sunken trench of PTSD.

Tears of joy or tears of sorrow, I have none to share today or tomorrow. This much I know: tears are a gift from my soul. They work their way up through my being to find release in my eyes, which are the windows to my soul.

"Oh God. My soul is not that bleak, is it?"

The possible answer terrifies me until my soul flashes a scriptural truth to my mind, which in turn flashes it to my heart, which immediately digests it. Once spiritually digested, my well-guarded heart opens its door to release the joyous peace that can only come from God's Word.[108]

Placing my hands once again on the trusty log, I affectionately pat it much like I would a trusty old dog. Then, lowering myself onto my knees, I pray.

"Lord, I've been up and down, twisted and bent, shuffling and crawling, tripping and falling my way through this trench day in and day out. For how long I do not know. But you do, and that's good enough for me."

Getting up and walking to the wall, I stop inches in front of it.

"Wow. Would you look at this?" I say in amazement, only to have my words echo back to me off the wall.

Stuffed into this wall were parchments made of animal skins and other substances unrecognizable to me. In awe, I stand before this ancient letterbox or prayer-gathering wall. Knowing I shouldn't but letting my curiosity get the best of me, I reach out for a dusty, crumbling parchment that partially protrudes from the wall above my head. When I touch this ancient document, part of it breaks off, falling to my feet.

"God, what have I done?"

Bending down, I reach out with trembling hands to pick this thing up. With these same trembling hands, I raise it up ever so gently and unfold it even more so. Lowering my head, I blow a few puffs of air on the parchment, watching history review itself for the first time.

"Oh Lord, is this ... is this ... is this ..."

Unable to finish speaking, I strain my eyes to focus in on the ancient writing.

"It's Hebrew of some sort."

Thinking back to my seminary days, I try recalling two years worth of Hebrew classes I struggled through. Then, almost dropping the parchment in excitement, I say, "I recognize this. I do. I do."

Pausing in amazement, I work my mind and eyes extra hard, drawing on my memory of a language I had major difficulties learning. There before my eyes, like the answers to a crossword puzzle, the words of the handwritten Hebrew script come to life in my mind, thrilling my heart.

> Have respect unto me, and pity me, for I am alone and poor. The troubles of my heart are enlarged; bring thou me out of my distresses. Look upon mine affliction and my trouble, and take away all my sins.[109]
>
> Psalm 25:16–18

I whisper a prayer of thanksgiving to the Lord as I refold the parchment, lowering it to the ground, gently placing it next to two folded notes at the wall's base. Moving my hand over to pick up much newer-looking notes, I stop just as my fingers feel the folded pieces of cardboard. Standing up, I leave the notes alone out of respect.

Placing my right hand respectfully on the wall and turning to look one more time upon the trusty, old, mossy log, I affectionately whisper, "Good-bye, new friends, and thank you." Turning and walking away never to look back, I wonder what was written on those two folded pieces of cardboard.

First note:

> God; it's me again, Johnny Boy. Just have a small request, the same one I had last week and the week before that. Bring back that Bob fellow. We need him, and he sure needs us. Come to think of it, God, I guess we all need you.
>
> Johnny Boy

Second note:

> God, I have been coming here for months. Thank you for bringing Bob here this day. Now watch over him, as he's in much pain. And keep him safe 'til I get back with some of the guys.
>
> Johnny Boy

AFFLICTION AND PAIN: SURVIVING PTSD'S DUAL LIFE

Look on my afflictions and my pain. And forgive
all my sins.

"How long has it been since I sat on that trusty old log?"
I thought out loud while shuffling in a zigzag motion
through some more difficult areas. That zigzagging got me
thinking about turns and u-turns in life. Such thoughts
brought an ever-growing smile to my face.

———————————

"Glad to see you smiling, Bob. But I am still waiting to
see a true smile. Come on. Show me those pearly whites,"
Cheryl teasingly taunts me to broaden my smile. I just
smile a bigger smile with closed lips. Then I reach over
the corner of the table to kiss her and kiss her again with
a more affectionate "I love you" kiss.

"We have had quite a journey together, haven't we?" I
say to Cheryl as I gaze into her eyes and steal another kiss.

"Now that's it. No more kisses. You stole enough
already," Cheryl laughingly says to me as I walk out the
back door.

Walking to my church office, I grin, reflecting on some of the silly situations I have gotten Cheryl into. As I reach for the worn handle of the church's back door, I laugh, watching my reflection on the door's window.

Opening the door, I walk through the threshold and down the hallway, nearly jumping out of my skin when the slowly closing church door shuts. Instantly, in that very split second, I'm back on my Duster with my crew, returning fire on those who lobbed some mortars on our position of a small makeshift firebase.

Once again, the sights, sounds, smells, and feelings of those ten Nam months permeate my being, pushing out any resistance to their reclaiming of my life, for how long they dig in and fight for ground depends on how tired or refreshed I am at the time.

Reaching for another worn doorknob, I prepare to enter my church office doing battle with undeniably devoted friends of yesteryear. Standing in the open threshold to my office, I bow my head, clench my fists, and breathe deeply as I hold my ground in a battle no one can see, hear, feel, or participate in but me. Sometimes I lose, in which case I retreat out of the building to go elsewhere, anywhere, or I enter the office and slide into my chair as if sliding into the Duster's gunner seat.

"What a day," I say, getting out of my seat.

Stretching an extended stretch, I prepare for another long night as the sun sinks below the horizon, dazzling me with its colors. I tend to my responsibilities that must be accomplished before tending to my personal needs.

There never seem to be enough hours in a twenty-four-hour day.

"Gosh. That's cold," I say, washing up with cold water, after which I sit down outside with some of my family to eat a meal of ham and beans along with some peaches and a cracker or two from my C-rations. Sometimes we laugh and cut up together, but not tonight. "It's hard to laugh after a day like this one," I think out loud as the night sky darkens.

Later, looking at my watch, I whisper to my brother, "It's pushing midnight, and not much is happening."

He yawningly replies, "Yeah. That's good. Let's hope it stays that way."

As time ticks on, I'm looking forward to a couple hours of sleep that will be coming my way in an hour or so. My brother interrupts my silent thoughts by whispering in my right ear, "Did you see those?"

"See what?"

"I think I saw some flashes?"

"You did. Incoming."

Our fellow crewmembers dash through and among the deafening exploding mortar rounds, making it safely to our Duster, from which we return deadly fire.

I jump up to a sitting position, taking the blankets with me. My startled wife knows not to touch me. Cheryl lets me silently lie back down. Now it is her time to pull watch as she prays for and watches over me until dawn's light.

Later that morning, as on other such mornings, Cheryl gives me a wonderful gift: her silence.

Sitting in the silence of the moment, I look around, wondering if I will ever get out of this trench. Moving my arms, I place my elbows on my knees and bring my hands together to rest my chin on them.

Here I sit, reflecting on my dual life of veteran and husband, veteran and father, veteran and pastor, veteran and brother, and veteran and son. Two distinct lives meshed together as one, a meshed life very few war vets open to non-vets, including our families—or what's left of them.

Lifting my head, I stare off into infinity, losing myself in thoughts of my family and our love for each other. This causes me to stand up and speak into the shadowy grays that eventually give way to darkness.

"I am so undeserving of such a loving wife. I am so undeserving of such loving daughters."

Sitting back down to my previous posture, I continue in thought. Starting to relax, I let my guard down. That enables an unresolved issue to rise up, pushing its way further than ever before.

Jumping to my feet, I leap into action. Rigid as a metal fence post, I push the escapee back down into the locked chamber from which it escaped.

Prancing around, nearly tripping a few times, I come back to where I was sitting.

"I know what I have to do, Lord, just as I know this deep pain in my heart is of my own making."

Standing up again, this time to pray, I raise my head, then my arms, then my voice to God:

> Turn Yourself to me, and have mercy on me, for I am desolated and afflicted. The troubles of my heart have enlarged; bring me out of my distresses! Look on my afflictions and my pain. And forgive all my sins.
>
> Psalm 25:16–18

Standing with bowed head and arms by my side, I wait, for it is good to wait on and for the Lord.[110]

Then, as the Lord would have it, I fall to my knees, lowering my forehead until it touches the trench's cold, hard, damp floor. Closing my eyes and clenching my hands together on the back of my neck, I simply let God have his way.

Repressed memories rush forth, skipping about like calves from the stall. Then God's Spirit cuts loose the nearly forty years of shackled feelings that burst out of my heart, rejoicing in the freedom that should have been theirs all along.

I nearly wept.

Then there she was, clear as clear could be, she who once cried out, "Where's my baby? Where's my baby?"; she who would nurse me through life-threatening illnesses; she who would spend long hours encouraging me through long sessions of hard-to-learn homework; she who would teach me the deep truths of prayer, just as her mother taught her; she who would spend time listening to my joys and sorrows followed by us praying together and searching the Scriptures for strength and courage; she who would see me, her only son, off to the army then off to war; she who would pray me through that war and life thereafter and eventually for my wife and children until that day on her deathbed she closed her eyes to open them in heaven.

———————————————

Grace, who, full of God's graces toward me, her loving son, remained just as gracious, if not more so after I came back from Vietnam disguised as her once-loving son. Gone were the days we would share our thoughts and concerns together in order to pray for each other and to encourage one another through God's Word. Gone were the peaceful nights snuggled in God's arms, tucked away in the safety of an abode called home.

Gone forever was the son once known to her as Bobby. Standing before Grace then and forty years later by her deathbed was Nam vet Robert, who successfully fought off all her attempts to infiltrate his well-guarded and defended heart, a heart that was hardened on the anvil of war by the fierce blows of PTSD, much like metal being shaped into a horseshoe on an anvil by a skilled blacksmith.

My mother carried Nam for nearly forty years, as have I. She passed from this world to her heavenly reward,[111] leaving behind a long-fought battle, a battle not of her own making but forced upon her when she daringly rose up in its face to pray me through it, a battle she courageously fought on her knees before her Savior and King, Jesus.

God, in his wonderfully unfathomable love, brought into my life another courageous woman of faith.[112] Cheryl never knew the Bobby whom Grace knew except on rare occasions when Nam vet Robert lets his guard down.

During these rare, all-too-short times, Cheryl smiles, daring to rejoice in thoughts and hopes that someday Bobby will gain strength and courage to battle against a mighty, thus-far-undefeatable foe, a deadly foe that has captured and brutalized millions and billions of warriors down through the ages, oftentimes taking their families as spoils of war, that foe being PTSD.

This foe has been called by many different names in many different cultures down through the centuries. After all these centuries it has come to be known throughout the world as Post Traumatic Stress Disorder.

PTSD, as a foe, started a secret war against me while I served my nation during an undeclared war in Vietnam. Vietnam was a place with very long, dark nights.

Looking at my watch and then looking toward the east, I yearn for the rising of the sun and with it, the rising hope of an equally uneventful day. Then I look toward my friend, saying, "A long night it has been, my friend."

"Yes. Thankfully, an uneventful one at that," he replies. Then he encourages me to rest my eyes for twenty minutes as he mans the M60 machine gun.

Listening to him, I yawn while placing my M79 grenade launcher across my lap. Then, closing my eyes to Vietnam's night skies, I dream of Chicago's often-smoggy nights.

I open my eyes after what seemed to be a long, deep sleep stretching far beyond twenty minutes. Startled at my surroundings, I look for my fellow guard and for my grenade launcher that should be on my lap. But what I see is a disarranged desktop and across my lap a Bible with its pages opened to Psalm 25.

ENEMIES AMONG US: BUT THERE IS A TABLE

> Consider my enemies, for they are many; and they hate me with cruel hatred.

Sitting up, I twist my legs out from underneath my damp, sticky makeshift sheet, placing my feet on the dirt floor. Just as my feet are securely on the bunker's floor, I feel the distinct feet of a rat scurrying over the top of my much-larger human feet.

"Another rat," I grumble under my breath as I quickly bring my legs and trespassed-against feet back under my poncho cover. Looking around, seeing nothing but hearing two distinctively different breathing rhythms of my fellow crew members, I know all is well.

I whisper a prayer for my two fellow sleeping crew members and my two other crew members pulling watch on our Duster. And before drifting back to sleep, I pray for my sister track's crew, who are doing the same thing we are presently doing. Last of all, I thank God for keeping me safe thus far and for watching over my family.

"Watching over you," I think out loud in a whisper. "I never thought of God watching over me and my loved ones as we watch over each other here, along with those under our protection." After thinking about that rat, I drift to sleep, thinking of God watching over us.[113]

"Preacher. Preacher."

"Yep? Is it that time all ready?"

"Sure is. Now get your butt out there so I can get some sleep. Oh, by the way, something's a-stirring out there, so be alert. I'd like to see tomorrow," my sergeant says as he turns underneath his poncho cover, quickly drifting into a restless sleep.

Finding my way through the pitch black, damp, smelly, somewhat livable and safe bunker is easy. All one does is follow the same routine twice a night every night as long as we are on this particular LZ.

Making it safely and quietly to the Duster, I whisper my crew member's name, followed by, "It's me, Preacher."

"Yep. I hear you," he whispers back, never breaking his alert scanning of the darkness and listening for anything out of place. Climbing up and into the Duster's open tub, I slide into my gunner's seat to pull my second two-hour shift of the night.

Looking at my watch, I rub my eyelids while pushing back a yawn. "One and a half hours before the rest get up," I whisper.

"Yep, and it won't even be light yet. Man, I'd give anything for one decent night's sleep," my fellow crew member whispers back, never dropping his fixed gaze into the darkness. There we sit fully alert yet yearning to be elsewhere.

Elsewhere sounds nice, I think to myself while scanning the shadows of the night for movement and listening to the jungle's nighttime sounds for noises out of place. I watch and listen for Viet Cong, who are masters at moving ever so slowly and just as quietly through any terrain to get to their objectives.

Seeing movement, I prepare myself to do what is necessary while saying, "Wow. Look at those little guys move," a few seconds later unleashing what I think is justifiable killing when they get too close to my position.

"Bobby, what did they ever do to you for you to do that to them?" my father, a WWII Veteran, asks me, his five-year-old son, as he sits down next to me. He went on to explain ant colonies and how each ant had its individual purpose to fulfill.

I sat spellbound there next to my father, who very seldom spoke, listening as I never listened before. From that day forward I viewed those little workaholics God made with a purpose to fulfill through my father's eyes: a wonder to behold.

"What's the purpose behind them doing that?" we ask our chief, who, with us, is standing in disbelief after witnessing the shooting of an unarmed VC. Come morning, we are glad to mount up on our Dusters to get off that small, isolated fire base.

"At least it wasn't by our hands or the hands of fellow Americans," I say extra loudly over the roar of the engine just behind us, the racket of the metal tracks under us, and the rapidly moving air hitting our faces and ears as our two Dusters set out on another mission.

Another crew member shouts back over all the noise, "Still, it doesn't justify the killing, even if it was a Viet Cong."

"To this day, I still think of a murder I witnessed while in Vietnam," I said, staring a thousand-yard stare.

"That must have been before my time," says a new-found old section member.

Three of us there, sitting around a shared table, remembering a shared life forty years earlier; that was when we were young in a faraway land, in a war that has never been far away from us.

Ever since leaving Vietnam, I have prayed a prayer that God took over thirty-five years to answer, the prayer being to meet up with former crew members who, for ten months, became closer than brothers. Since we all went by nicknames, I have no clue how to contact any of them. I simply have to wait on God.

"Walking and thinking while I think and walk. Now that's something to think about!" Walking a little bit farther, I say, "What am I thinking?" Then I stop to think about what I'm thinking about.

After thinking about it, I decide to just stand still to listen for and to the voice of the Lord,[114] and to enjoy waiting on him here in this trench in the bottom of the valley of the shadow of death.

After standing for a very long time, my mind starts to wander with my soul in hot pursuit. Then my heart, which can be desperately wicked at times,[115] cheers on my mind. Immediately my conscience rises up, yelling down my heart while cheering on my soul. Wow! What a rush!

Before I know it, there's a thunderous applause that is overtaken by an eruption of voices chanting, "Go mind.

Go mind. Put your mind into it. Go mind. You can do it. Go mind."

Not to be outdone, there is an explosion of dazzling lights from the fellowship of the saints lighting the way for my soul to catch up to my stumbling mind. Upon the soul's glorious tackle of the renegade mind, an earthshaking, wind-producing, ear-piercing chorus of "Hallelujah" burst down from the heavens above.

This gets me jumping up to my feet, at which time they both yell with all their toes telling my lungs to kick in high gear. With one, two, three deep breaths, my lungs command my legs to rocket off in a run for their lives.

Wham, goes the back of my head on the trench's floor when my legs jet out my body from a standing position. Man, am I flying (after stabilizing myself) across this trench's floor, nearly running over my humiliated mind and victorious soul.

"Wow! This is great!" I yell, waking myself up from a nap. "Oh no. Get yourself back to sleep to dream another dream," I tell myself. But I do not listen. Why? For fear of a nightmare that would be equally dreadful as my previous dream was delightful, thus a common enemy many war veterans of all wars down through the ages and across cultural lines have: sleep.

I walk forward again, as always with the Word of God that is "a lamp unto my feet and a light unto my path."[116] Grinning as I press forward, thinking on the lessons of my humorous dream, I pray, "Thank you, God. You truly do move in mysterious and wonderful ways."

After what seems to have been a long trek, I find a place to sit to rest in the Lord. Such a rest for me has always been to soak in God's presence through quiet time in his Word, the Bible. For how long I was there I do not know. But this I do know: I was refreshed as only God's Word stimulated by his Spirit can do.

Getting up with a psalm in my heart, I start quoting the Twenty-third Psalm:

> The Lord is my shepherd: I shall not want. He maketh me to lie down in green pastures: he leadeth me beside the still waters. He restoreth my soul: he leadeth me in the paths of righteousness for his name's sake. Yea, thou I walk through the valley of the shadow of death, I will fear no evil: for thou art with me, thy rod and thy staff they comfort me.
>
> Psalm 23 (KJV)

As I quote verse five ("Thou preparest a table before me in the presence of mine enemies: thou anointest my head with oil: my cup runneth over"), the voice of the Lord speaks forth: "I prepare a table before you in the presence of your enemies: I anoint your head with oil. Your cup runs over."

Just then, the glory of the Lord shone about, lighting up the trench in the bottom of the valley of the shadow of death, and with it bringing to light a fabulous table, a table fit for royalty, a table on which sat a polished cup with what seemed to be duller imprints resembling fingers of hands. There was also a flask of oil.

I marvel at such a sight that was beyond my meager description. Then, even more marvelously, I hear the King gently call out my name.

Then, with a smile, the most beautiful smile I've ever seen, he says, "Come, Robert, to this table I have set for you."

Being captivated in awe, I never notice or hear the insults and angry threats of all my soul's enemies. But there they are, in the shadows and darkness, watching the King of kings and Lord of lords bless one of his servants— I might add, the least of them all.

All I can think or do is acknowledge my deep gratitude for a blessing so undeserved. This gives way to a silent question: "Is this for and about me because of what I have done for Jesus?"

To this I hear an instant rebuttal: "'Your sins were washed away at Golgotha.'[117] 'Your soul was set free in the empty tomb.'[118] 'Your future resurrection was guaranteed at Bethany on the 'Mount of Olives.'[119] 'Your empowerment by and protection in and sealing of the Holy Spirit were set in motion at Pentecost.'[120] 'And your placement in the Body of Christ was declared by me before the foundations of the world.'[121] 'It never has been about you, but about me fulfilling my Father's will.'[122] 'He, who at the appointed time,[123] sent me as a means of atonement for your sins and the sins of the world.'[124] 'Sadly, many are called but few are chosen.'[125] 'You did not choose me, I chose you.'[126] So, Robert, here you are. Come, for all things are ready."

Upon these words there is a great shuffling of chairs. To my amazement, there they are again, the hosts of saints. Sitting among them are my loving wife and daughters, who, like me, were saved by the "precious blood of the Lamb."[127] I stand in awe before humbly approaching the table set for me in the presence of my enemies.

And I am blessed as I bless the Host of the table. Then, here among the saints, I smile the most beautiful smile of all.

DELIVERANCE AND TRUST GO HAND IN HAND

Oh, keep my soul, and deliver me; let me not be ashamed, for I put my trust in You.

"This feels good," I say, stretching myself out on a bench after a hot meal of salisbury steak and mashed potatoes along with some veggies and fruit topped off with a piece of cake and a candy bar from my C-rations. I gaze upward into the starry host while its splendor shines downward toward me.

Lying peacefully atop a makeshift bench of worn, hardened sandbags, I eventually surrender to sleep, disregarding deadly dangers lurking a few yards beyond. I whisper a prayer just prior to drifting into a long-awaited one and a half hours of sleep. It's a prayer that unites my frazzled mind and heart with my hopeful soul and steadfast spirit within a twenty-year-old body.

This prayer was taught to me and prayed over me until I could join in praying it. This prayer is the same prayer millions upon millions of parents and grandparents were taught by their parents and grandparents, who were taught by their parents and grandparents, who were taught by their...

Now I lay me down to sleep. I pray the Lord my soul to keep. If I die before I wake, I pray the Lord my soul to take. Amen.

After waking up from a late afternoon nap, I set out busying myself trying to find something to do. I walk around the state park's campground twice before finding a stump on a ledge overlooking an inlet of the Missouri River.

Here I sit on this stump under the hot South Dakota sun. Looking at my feet is all I can think to do at the moment. Continuing to look down at my feet, I start kicking up some loose pebbles, eventually making a game of it to pass time.

I do not know how long I've been sitting here watching these small pebbles bounce into gentle tumbles before coming to slow stops. Each pebble, upon stopping, leaves a funny little trail in the dusty ground. These little trails trigger a memory, which shoots me back through time, back to the very moment God used some of his tiniest servants to teach this big servant an unforgettable lesson.

I was lying on my bunk in Fort Hood, Texas, bored to tears, needing something to do to kill time. I noticed a column of ants moving past my bunk. Reminding me of a column of tanks, that column of ants inspired what I thought to be a good game. Being a tank driver, I thought I would change functions and become a gunner. So there I was, killing time by killing ants, lowering the boom on those little unsuspecting creatures by scrunching them with my finger. One by one, I wiped them out. One by one, I sent those little creatures to ant heaven.

I was about to lower the boom on a defiant ant that dared to move forward to the front of the column of dead ants when I heard a voice behind me say, "Robert, what would you do if that was a human being?" I stopped and looked at my fingertip, which was full of ant legs and other parts, and then turned to see who was talking to me.

I saw no one there, so I surmised that it was the Lord speaking to me. I looked back down at the column of dead ants and at my fingertip and said, "Lord, I would not do that." About three hours later, my Top (First Sergeant) walked into my barrack bay and started reading the names of those going to "vacation wonderland (Vietnam)."

One of my friends, a sergeant, upon hearing his name, started to yell. Then he started to curse and suddenly burst into tears, followed by more yelling and cursing. He did not want to go back to Vietnam.

Top had come in to read off names many times before that particular day, but I never thought I would be going to Vietnam, because I was the sole surviving son of my family. But just a few hours after hearing the Lord's piercing question, my name was called. I was on my way to Vietnam.

Now I'm stuck in a quagmire of thoughts, dreams, and desires intermixed with hopelessness, fears, and doubts along with faith, hope, and love. Emotionally sinking fast, I grasp at anything that'll help rescue me.

The first stick of unfulfilled dreams snaps. Next, the large branch of nagging doubts ensnares me in its submerged portions. Finally, with all options gone, I reach out to grab hold of a small, green leaf, thinking as I do so, *At least I go down holding something pretty.*

But go down I do not. The little leaf is attached to a thick sapling that grew up out of a large, strong root, a root that eventually was covered by this sinking sand. This massive root protruded out from a distant mighty oak tree, a tree resembling a centurion standing ready to do what it needs to do at the moment it needs to do it.

Climbing up and out of my once-sinking death, I crawl to the security of the mighty oak. Lying there at the foot of this majestic tree, I fall asleep.

"Hey, Preacher, are you okay over there?" one of my crew members asks me from a distance.

"Sure am. It's a great day, isn't it?" I reply from where I'm sitting on a ledge high above the peaceful countryside. Seeing no danger and losing myself in peaceful thoughts, I pull out my Bible from the utility pocket on my right pant leg. "Such peace," I think out loud.

Suddenly, pressure in my head rushes upward, coming to a peak right above my scalp as a sniper's bullet splits my hair. In one move, I throw myself backward, twisting my torso until my face hits the dirt. From there, I low crawl back to the Duster faster than I've ever crawled before. While crawling, I pray, "Thank you, God, for saving my life. And please forgive me for being so stupid in the first place."

Once next to the safety of the tried and proven Duster, I jump to my feet only to discover I jumped up from a stump in South Dakota. Wiping my sweaty brow, I look around to see if anyone saw me. Even if they did, they never saw what I just experienced in a flashback followed by a dream that triggered another flashback.

Man, what a rush! I think to myself, walking back to the campsite. The rest of the afternoon and night were full of activities of unseen actions taking place in my heart, mind, and my body itself as I went through adrenalin withdrawal.

Late that night, after my family is safely tucked away in our three-room camping tent, I slip out. Still dealing with the effects of the adrenalin rush followed by the adrenalin withdrawal, I make my rounds. Once again, I do what I have done every night since those nights in a faraway land, in a war that is never far away from me: I watch.

INTEGRITY: LEARNING THE TRUTH ABOUT TRUTH

Let integrity and uprightness preserve me, for I wait for You.

Anything worth learning is worth time spent within its basics. "Now that's quite a thought. Let's see if I can still get it straight. Let's see now. 'Anything worth learning is worth time spent within its basics.' Yes, I got it."

Yes, Robert, but do you know what it means? flashes through my mind while pricking my soul and penetrating my heart.

Looking around, I say, "Here we go again," while rubbing the back of my neck. *I know what this means,* I think, hoping all the time I'm wrong. But this late in my life, after walking in the Lord for most of it, I know what's coming: a test from above in how well I live out the basic truths within the Word of God.[128]

"Now, Bobby, are you telling me the truth?" my elementary school teacher asks of me while looking at me from behind her desk.

"Why, of course I am," I say, staring back at her with one of my best convincing, truthful looks drawn up from my heart.

Then the battle of wits begins between me and this obviously amateur competitor in the art of staring down the other person.

Hey, she's better than she lets on, I think to myself as I turn up the notch of believability a click or two. Next, I send her down in defeat by applying my never-fail boyish grin. This is followed by the victory walk back to my desk.

All was as well as well could be until I walked through our back door into the kitchen. There I come face-to-face with Grandma, who usually greets me with a hug and kiss and cookies, good ole sweet Granny. But standing there this afternoon was the awesome, most victorious paddler of Chicago's southside: Grandma the great.

My previous victorious countenance evaporated nearly as fast as my turning maneuver to flee back through the door through which I had entered into the paddle zone, yelling, "Made it," while throwing open the back screen door, only to realize I was running in place. "Oh no. I should've worn suspenders."

There behind me was Grandma with paddle in one hand and my belt in the other. The drag to the bathroom was a long one, as I unsuccessfully tried to break free from her pants-belt-shirt hold.

The next day I walked into the classroom to face the rookie turned pro overnight. She and I had many a staredown after that, to which I went down every time, nearly wearing thin the paddle that awaited me at home.

Grandma about wore me out with that ominous paddle, which refused to break before my ornery behavior did. I just kept going with that staring down unrighteous behavior until I learned the truth about truth: truth is truth all the time.[129]

Stopping to catch my breath, I start smiling at the memory of my early childhood days of learning right from wrong and the importance of telling the truth and adhering to the moral compass of the Ten Commandments[130] and trusting the reliability of the Holy Scriptures.[131]

"I was a fortunate one," I said with a joyful voice to anyone who was listening down here in this trench.

Still laughing, I think back to my army boot camp days at Fort Jackson, South Carolina. One fateful night some of us acquired fresh, hot hamburgers from a fellow troop we paid to sneak out and buy them for us. Oh, how delicious they tasted right up to the moment the barrack bay lights flashed on and a menacing voice bellowed out, "Attention."

I and the other trespassers against the no-food law stuffed the remaining half-eaten burgers in our mouths. And like a hound dog treeing a raccoon, my DI stood right in front of me, nose to nose, yelling, "Swallow that, boy." Upon my rapidly chewing the half-eaten burger, he yelled out, "I said, 'Swallow,' not, 'Chew.'" I had indigestion for nearly two days.

Still laughing at myself while maneuvering around some difficult spots in this despicable trench of PTSD, I stumble, nearly falling headlong on jagged rocks. After catching my balance, I stand still, gazing around in all directions.

"Man, this is like a minefield of disastrous proportions," I yell while kicking one of the small boulders.

"It doesn't take much to get you upset, does it?"

Startled by the voice and even more so by the question, I jerk backward, nearly falling. Once again, I gaze around after catching my balance.

"Wow. A giddy person at that too, you are, aren't you?"

"Now this is getting annoying," I say while looking for the intruder in my laughable moments of joy.

"Over here, Sojourner. I am over here. Come join me if you'd like to. Company would be good right about now."

Maneuvering my way toward the voice, I start thinking about many of the difficulties Cheryl and I have encountered on our journey in life. Smiling, I think out loud, "But in and through them all, God took care of us by meeting our needs and sometimes giving us our hearts' desires.[132] We are blessed with two lovely and loving daughters who, with us, love the Lord."

"You're getting closer. Keep coming."

Turning a little to the left and walking a spell before turning back to the right, I zigzag between the jagged rocks toward the voice. While walking through this maze, I start thinking of our family's journey through life's maze of difficulties, blessings, illnesses, healings, tight financial situations, surprise gifts, fears, hurts, joys, sorrows, great adventures of faith, and much more. This gets me singing the old hymn "Count Your Blessings" while traversing my way through this maze toward the voice.

When this unseen person started to sing along with me, I knew I was getting close to him. Closing in on his position, I started anticipating some added joy of fellowshipping with another sojourner in this mess of a place.

"Well, greetings to you. Or should I say, 'Halt. Who goes there'?" rings clear in my ears.

Stopping in what seems to be an amphitheater made of boulders and rocks, I look around for the person talking to me. It should be easy to find him because for some reason unknown to me, this place has a warm glow likened to a child's nursery with a nightlight.

Looking upward, I cannot see the higher portions of the boulders through the darkness that shrouds them. I envision this guy perched like an eagle high above, looking down far below.

"Thank you for calling me over here to you in this unique place," I say while turning slowly in a circular motion as if searching out my perimeter. Then, continuing on, I ask, "By the way, what is this place? And where's this light coming from? Oh yeah. What's your name? Mine is Bob, Bob Scholten."

"Mike's my name, Sojourner. You do not mind me calling you that, now do you?"

"No, Mike. I do not mind at all. I guess I am a sojourner because I have been traveling through this trench ever so long." After saying that, I respond to my own words as if surprised by them.

"Got yourself, didn't you? You are not the first. Nor will you be the last," Mike says, perched up high there in his chair, never breaking his eaglelike stare from scanning far and wide for other sojourners like me. "You will need some rest, Sojourner. I mean really rest yourself up good, Robert."[133]

"Why? Am I going somewhere, Mike?"

"You sure are," Mike says to me through the darkness. "You are going that way, to your left, when you leave here. And I must warn you, for that is why I am here. You are about to enter some of the toughest and most hostile terrain in this trench life you and I have in common. And leave you must."

"What do you mean by ..."

"Robert, I said what I said. And what I said is what I said. You will go that away when you leave me here as you found me, alone but not alone. You know what I mean by that, do you not?"

"If you are referring to the times in Nam during which I pulled guard duty, alone on watch by myself, yes, I do know what you mean. I was not alone, for the Lord my God was with me and within me.[134] Thus, I was not alone."

"See, Robert. I knew you knew. Now get yourself up here and rest by my side as I watch."

"Before I do that, Mike, please tell me how you know this. You know, how bad it is out there where you say I must go."

"Because me and my men made it through, most of them that is."

I reply with a lump in my throat, "Most of them?"

"Yes, Sojourner. I said most of them. And let me tell you, it wasn't easy at all, not one bit. In fact, there were some who never made it. They simply gave up, and that was it. There were others who wandered off the beaten path, looking for an easier way. Never did see them again. Then there were those who were simply overcome by fear and anxiety. They took off on us and scattered in all directions. It's really spooky some nights here on watch, when I think I hear their distant moans and groans and sometimes their curses."

"If it is really that bad," I inquire of him, "why did you come back through it? I would have stayed on the other side. I really would have, never to look back. I just don't understand what possessed you to come back through it."

"Oh, I think you do, my friend. In fact, someday you might do the same thing. Yes. You or whoever else God chooses. Whoever it is will come back for the same reason I did."

"And what's that, may I ask?"

"To pull watch, my friend. Someone will come back through that grievous, terrible place to relieve whoever is pulling watch at that time. Together, they will encourage each other. And together, they will watch a spell, 'til he or she greets the new watch farewell and heads back through it to the other side."

Startled at what this guy is saying to me, I reply by saying, "God would really have to change my mind and my heart in order to do such a thing as that." Pausing in disbelief and shock at his words, I just stare up into the darkness that shrouds him. Finally, after some time of puzzlement, I continue talking to him by saying, "My goodness, man. I don't even want to think about that. I have been through enough already."

"Now, Robert, have you really been through so awful much? Or does it just seem that way to you? Think about that while you climb up here to sit a while with me. Come on, Sojourner Robert. The view is awesome. In fact, you will not believe your eyes."

The climb is long and hard.

Just as I am giving up, Mike says, "There's a ledge a few feet above you on which you can rest."

Reaching the ledge, I look up through the grayish shadows to see Mike dressed in what seems to be WWII or Korean-era clothing. He is sitting on what resembles a comfortable chair worn into a rock through centuries worth of people sitting in it. The large rock is nestled between two boulders.

Continuing my climb up and around and between boulders, I dare not look down. Finally arriving next to Mike, I plop myself down at his left side.

"Hey there, Robert. You can open your eyes now. You are quite safe up here. You need not fear falling. Just open your eyes and take it all in."

Thinking out loud, I say, "Take what in? There's nothing out there but grievous shadows giving way to darkness giving way to misery."

"Now listen. Do I need to reach over and open your eyelids for you?"

Grabbing hold of Mike's left arm and placing my left hand in a cleft of the rock behind me and firmly placing my feet on the boulder beneath me, I slowly open my eyes.

"Wow! How long is it like this?" I ask in total disbelief of the crystal clear skies lighting up the trench below and the valley of the shadow of death above.

"Robert, my friend, it is like this as long as I sit in this seat, in this rock, nestled in between these two boulders."

"Really? What protects you, Mike?"

"Why, Robert, how could you ask such a question that you already know the answer to? You know the answer, for it is within your heart, right where it was etched by the Lord of all himself."

"What? What did you say? Did you say what I think you said?"

"Come on, Robert. There you go again. You really are a funny guy. You know that? Now clear your mind and search your soul and repeat what you know with me."

In doing what I am instructed to do, a smile breaks forth on my face as I let go of Mike's arm and drop my left arm to my side. Laughing like a child discovering the ability to say a new word, I speak in unison with Mike, "Let integrity and uprightness preserve me, for I wait for you."

CAMP REDEEMER'S REST

Redeem Israel, O God, out of all their trouble.

So far so good, I say to myself, finally making it to the bottom of the huge boulder formation. Bowing my head in prayer, I am overcome with an urge to kneel. In doing so, I feel what seems to be thick, hard wood underneath me. Rocking backward up onto my feet, entering into a squatting position, I begin looking around to see what kind of wood this is.

"So you found it, did you, Sojourner? Spend as much time as you need examining it, Robert. Do not feel as you have to rush out of there like many other people do."

Following instructions is a lesson I am learning during this unwelcoming journey in PTSD. So, listening to Mike's advice, I spend time here in this part of the amphitheater.

After much time growing frustrated with myself, I say, "All I am doing is sitting here, twiddling my thumbs and growing more bored by the minute." Continuing twiddling my thumbs, anger raising from my heart. This I take notice of and pray, *Lord, I am growing angry. I know this is not good and only leads to trouble. I confess to you my wayward mind and need of renewing it through the trans-forming power of your Word.*[135]

Standing up, I take a deep breath, holding it as long as I can and then slowly releasing it. "This feels good," I say out loud. Breathing and exhaling a second time, I notice something I was missing during my pity party. "Wow! How did I miss this? It's so obvious. These beams are made out of cedar trees."

"It took you longer than some folks and shorter than others to discover this fact. Now start anew your journey through the trench of PTSD, remembering what I told you. Also search the Word of God pertaining to cedar. What you learn will help you immensely. God bless you, Sojourner Robert."

God has blessed me greatly, in more ways than I can count. He has delivered me from death's door more than once. He has filled my life with faith, hope, and love and has given me opportunities to use these three great gifts for his glory.[136] He has blessed me with three families: my wife and two daughters, along with our extended family; my church family, along with all fellow Christians; and my family of fellow veterans.

Thinking on my blessing, I lose track of time again. Some mornings I awake not knowing what days of the week they are. Other mornings I force myself out of bed, fighting my way through the day by pushing back PTSD's constant advances.

This internal battle involves my whole being. Thus, by late morning I'm ready to give in or my body is pumping itself full of adrenalin. If not careful, I'll go off like an untied balloon set free from a child's hand.

"Man, am I tired," I say with a long face and even longer sigh. This portion of the trench has been difficult for me to maneuver through. I try unwinding but cannot because of all the commotion around me. It seems as though I am wandering in some kind of intersection between the trench of PTSD and the valley of the shadow of death and the pathway above the valley.

I leave in search of a secluded place to be alone in my thoughts and prayers. "This looks like a good secluded spot," I think out loud.

It is here in my seclusion that I fight another battle, one of resisting PTSD's hideous attempts at making me hide in isolation rather than refreshing myself with restful thoughts and activities. Today, it's a battle I win. Therefore, my family also wins, as does my congregation.

In this win-win setting, I face God in the midst of my brokenness through prayer. Gathering up the shattered pieces of my life, I surrender anew to the Lord's will for my life and my family and my ministry. In this, my humility, God gently reshapes me much like a master craftsman reshapes a lump of clay on a spinning wheel.[137]

Around and around I go, faster and faster I go, smoother and smoother I become as God shapes me with his redeeming hands into a vessel/person of his choosing. He is forever smoothing out hard lumps of stubbornness in my life. He is squeezing out hidden air pockets of addictions. He is moisturizing out hairline fractures of anger. He is scraping out gritty spots of dishonesty. He is digging out stones of long-held grudges. Plus, there is so much more work to be done in me on his spinning wheel.

Thinking about the spinning wheel, I mumble, "Work. I used to work. Now I just work at working, which doesn't always work out. My life used to mean something. Now I just wander around in meaninglessness, trying to recover what I once had. My searching is futile because what I once had no longer exists. It fled from me like dust flees from a dusty sidewalk on a windy day. So what's the use of continuing on in such a sorry state? Solomon was right. Vanity. Vanity. All is vanity. In fact, this is what I am go—"

I am interrupted in midsentence when God's Spirit snatches me out of my self-induced pity party, plopping me back on the Master Potter's spinning wheel.

"Oh no! Not again!" I yell while zigzagging on the wheel, trying to escape the Master's hands. Huffing and puffing, I cry out, "This running is in vain. Feet, get me out of here," as I pour out all my energy into running rapidly decreasing circles as God's moistened hands close in on me.

After a few extra spins on the spinning wheel and a few extra squeezes in the Potter's hands, I am released with a few less lumps, air pockets, fractures, grit, and stones. It reminds me of Paul and Florence Hudson, who, in 1979, introduced us to their apple orchard in North Carolina. Paul instructed Cheryl and me in the art of pruning apple trees.

Paul divided the small orchard between the four of us. "Now, Bob, you have to cut the branches like I showed you. Can you do that?" Paul asks me.

"Sure. I can do that. Nothing to it," I reply with a grin but down deep wondering why he only asked me and not Cheryl or his wife, Florence. I found out about an hour later, when Paul returned to my excellently pruned section of the orchard.

"What have you done, Robert? It's been an hour, and there are only small clippings on the ground. Where are the pruned branches?" Paul asks while shaking his head in disbelief.

"But, Mr. Hudson, I just couldn't butcher these trees like you showed me. If I did, there would hardly be any apples on them. And you know my love for apples."

"Oh, for heaven's sake, Bob. I'll show you how these trees will give us a bumper harvest of apples. Give me your clipper and pruning knife. Now watch."

I about died when Mr. Hudson started cutting off extended branches. All I could think about were the apple pies and apple dumplings and cooked apples and sliced apples being cut out of existence. I was absolutely shocked at the sight of such butchery of potential desserts.

Months later, near Thanksgiving, Cheryl and I received a letter from the Hudsons. Enclosed in the envelope were incredible pictures of their apple orchard. There in my hands was the evidence of Paul Hudson's knowledge of apple trees and the important art of pruning.

Paul made a believer of me regarding the managing of an orchard to assure a bountiful harvest. He and Florence also brought to life in Cheryl's and my mind the importance of God pruning us so we would produce more fruit.[138] Now I hope my life is producing baskets of fresh fruit for the Lord's delight.

Laying down my basket of freshly picked apples, I sit under a large tree with my back up against its massive trunk. There next to the basket full of freshly picked apples, I drift to sleep with a breeze of fresh air caressing my face, filling my nostrils with even sweeter aromas. Deeper and deeper into sleep I go until reaching that well-guarded and secured few minutes of blissful dreamlessness.

Coming out of deep sleep, I pass through dreams, trying to guard myself against lurking nightmares waiting to destroy what sweet rest I have remaining.

"Oh, how I love this sweet, fresh air," I say while reaching for an apple from my basket, only to start coughing up the stale air of the trench. Totally disorientated, I lean over toward the basket of apples only to discover a pile of stones next to me.

"This is disgusting," I say in disbelief of what I have woken up to. "At least the tree is real," I mumble.

Still sitting here, I pick up stones to throw at a dilapidated sign a stone's throw from my tree. Every stone I throw misses its mark as if that old sign was protected somehow.

"Good grief. This can't be happening," I say, getting up to my feet with a fistful of stones.

Walking toward the decrepit sign, I drop the stones, shaking my head in disgust at its message: "Welcome to the trench of PTSD. May your journey be long, lousy, and disgusting until you drop into its only exit: your grave."

"Now doesn't that beat all?" I softly say while taking the sign in my hands, shaking and twisting it feverishly until I drop from exhaustion.

Seeing it still there in front of me, I calmly rise to my feet, taking the lousy sign in my hands for another bout of fierce shaking and twisting with added punches and kicks. Once again, I wind up exhausted on the ground at the feet of the intact sign.

Getting up for another round with the sign, I yell at it, "Oh no you don't."

But it did.

"Maybe I ought to be praying about this," I finally say to myself between breaths.

So I do, and in so doing, I calm down. In calming down, I begin to think more clearly. And in thinking more clearly, I come up with an idea. My idea involves cedar.

It's difficult working because injustices abound in this place, hurting to the core. Ingratitude lingers everywhere, acting like a poison sickening my spirit. Apathy adds to the darkness of this place like a damp, mildewed wool blanket. It is easy to give up on my idea and all the labor pertaining to it.

I am growing tired but keep working toward finishing this project in hope that all who experience it will find refreshment and encouragement within its truth.[139]

"Lord, I need help. I am in way over my head. At the rate I'm going, you best keep me alive 'til I am a hundred and five. Ouch! I'm surprised I still have a thumb," I grumble after hitting it with a hammer. "Where's my help?" I yell, throwing the hammer out of the hollowed-out tree I just cut through with ax, hatchet, hammer, and chisel.

"That must have hurt."

"Great. Now I'm hearing voices in my head. Next I'll be seeing things. What's after that?" I sarcastically say out of frustration.

"Usually a psych ward."

"Oh, now that's funny, Lord, real funny," I think out loud as I sit in the middle of my unfinished creation.

"So tell me, Sojourner Robert, what's with that sign over there? I tried knocking it down, but I wound up on the ground completely worn out."

"You're a good ventriloquist, Lord. You sound just like Mike," I whisper under my breath.

"What did you say?"

"You got to be kidding. You who read hearts and hear all prayers are asking me what I said?"

With that, I hear a hearty, loud laugh from behind me. Startled, I jump up and turn to see who is behind me.

"I can't believe it. Is that you, Mike? What are you doing here? Did someone relieve you of your watch?"

"Sure is. It is good to see you again after all these years. And, yes, God did send someone to relieve me. And she will do mighty fine up there pulling watch."

"All these years, you say?" I respond back to Mike. "Has it really been that long, my friend? I just can't believe it. On the other hand, this lousy trench sucks life right out of a person. And it gives nothing back but misery, gloom, and depression."

Mike walks into the hollowed-out tree to greet me with a smile and a handshake followed by a bear hug.

"You look tired, Robert. By the way, what are you doing here? It looks and smells fantastic." Mike, looking back toward the sign, says, "What a contrast to that miserable sign over there," pointing to it. He picks up some stones and throws them all, one at a time, at the sign. "How did I miss that crummy thing at such a close distance?"

Laughingly, I share with Mike my encounters with the sign and bring him up to date with my project. "So you see, Mike, this shelter is my response to that diabolical signpost that is rooted in hell."

"What a great idea, Bob. You do not mind me calling you Bob, now do you, Sojourner Robert? I love how you carved out one entrance in the shape of an open tomb and the other in the shape of a cross. What a message of redemption and hope all of us sojourners need to encounter and experience in this measurable trench of PTSD."[140] Looking around within the hollowed-out tree, he says, "Cedar. An excellent choice, Bob. It is self-preserving; aroma-producing; excellent for floors, walls, and ceilings. And, as you have discovered, it is great for carving."

I walk Mike to where I started carving letters into the smooth surface of the tree's hollowed-out hall. "As you can see, Mike, I'm not that good at carving words. It is my intention to carve out Psalm Twenty-five in large letters along this wall," I say, pointing to the wall and then gently running my hand over it. "Over closer to that entrance, I am trying to carve in Psalm Twenty-three. On that wall behind us," I say as I turn to face it, "I am trying to whittle out seats from it, with the wall being their backs."

We both walk through the cross entrance back into the stale air of the trench. We both immediately notice the difference and walk back into the hollowed-out cedar tree, where, once again, the lamp of the Lord lights up our path, which illuminates the hollowed-out hall.

"Bob, how can I put this? You did a fabulous job cutting through this magnificently large tree and smoothing the inside surfaces. But your carving and whittling skills are nonexistent."

"Well, thank you, Mike, for the compliment. But did you have to be so brutally honest about the other?"

"Nothing like the truth, Bob. There is nothing like the truth. Accept it, Bob. And please accept my offer to finish those chairs and benches for you and carve the Twenty-third and Twenty-fifth Psalms into the walls for you."

"Yes, there is nothing like the truth. And I do accept it, for I know a carver I'm not," I answer, dropping my much-worn pocketknife. "But, Mike, do you really know what you're getting into?" I ask him in all sincerity.

"Look at me, Bob. I forgot how hideously hard that portion of trench was that I just came through. I know my limits. I cannot go through much more. So here I stop. And here I have a purpose that will help all those who follow after us to this point. By the way, I made furniture from hickory and cedar before being drafted. So a carver I am, Bob."

Mike makes a lot of sense to me. The thought of leaving is bittersweet. I invested a lot in this project, and part of me wants to see it through. But then Nam is hot on my heels and heavy on my shoulders. It is past time to leave. I have been in one place way too long. Once again, I ready myself to run. Once again, my family will be pulled up from their home and friends as I dart elsewhere, with my family hanging on for dear life by their prayers and love.

" Hey, Sojourner. Look at me."

"Excuse me. What did you say?"

"I said, 'Look at me.' You have that thousand-yard stare about you. Listen to me and listen well. Be sure you leave for the right reason. Did you hear anything I just said?"

"Mike, I got to get out of here. This place is eating me up."

"Eating you up? Sojourner Robert, look at what you have accomplished here, you and your family. Stay and help me help you finish this…this…what is this, anyway? What shall we call it?"

Shifting my weight from one foot to the other while looking at the huge cedar tree, I respond with a shaky voice, "This, Mike, is a shelter from the storm.[141] It is a haven from the persecutor.[142] It is a resting place from the pursuer.[143] This is Camp Redeemer's Rest."

"Yes. That's it, Bob. It cannot be anything else but Camp Redeemer's Rest."

Facing the tree with our backs to the sign, we lift our arms in praise to the Lord, who is our Redeemer, and quote Psalm 25:22 together: "Redeem Israel, O God, out of all their trouble."

"Mike, let's turn verse twenty-two into a prayer for all of us veterans from all countries and of all wars."

"Let's do it," Mike says excitedly. "If you do not mind, I'd love to pray standing in this doorway shaped like Christ's open tomb while you pray in the doorway shaped like Christ's cross."

"Let's do it," I say with a broken voice. "I will begin, and then you come in, and then I, and then you. And we'll close together with a hearty 'amen.' Dear gracious Lord God Almighty, hear our prayer on behalf of our fellow veterans and families we lift to you from this trench of PTSD."

"We who travel this sunken trench have our share of troubles that have roots in the seedbed of war. These troubles are still with us because their root systems are following us wherever we go, weaving themselves among our personal and family roots. We are tired of the oppressive fruit these intertwined roots are producing and feeding in our lives and in our families."

"Please, Lord, untangle these roots, for we cannot. Then encourage us to deal with the sour fruit of war in our lives that have been nurtured by PTSD. Set all free from that which oppresses us, and gently lift us all who seek refuge in you from the depths of depression."

"We acknowledge bringing back violence of war in our hearts, thinking and believing we could rid ourselves of it once back home. Lord, some of us have been able to do so, while others of us have not. We all need your gentle touch in our lives and relationships. Forgive us our sins of anger, and help us to forgive those who have sinned against us through their angry hearts. And please forgive all of us who, at one time or another, raised angry fists heavenward toward you."

"War sickens the soul. This we know. You heal the soul. This we also know.[144] We earnestly pray for your healing touch in all of our lives, which have been exposed to war's harsh realities."

"Lord, free us captives from the tyranny of PTSD. Help us then help our fellow veterans and families deal with lifelong healing processes from our internal and external wounds of captivity in PTSD's dungeons of terror and agony."

"Many of us who sojourn in this trench have faced death more times than we wish to remember. Some of us took life, and some of us let it live on. All of us have been touched by the cold, hideous fingers of death as we run from its ever-present desire to grab and drag us down into the grave. Some of us grew tired of this chase and gave in by taking ourselves out. Lord, have mercy on us. Cleanse our wounds and comfort our sorrows. Forgive our sins and set us free through your Son,[145] who alone is Lord of lords and King of kings forever and ever."

"Amen and amen. So be it, Lord. Amen."

After our prayer, we meet in the middle of the hollowed hall of cedar. Mike has tears running down his cheeks. I have none. We both extend our hands and grab hold of each other's shoulders for one last bear hug, knowing it will be our last.

"You take care of your family," Mike says to me.

I respond with, "You take care of Camp Redeemer's Rest." With one final handshake, I walk out of the hollowed-out cedar tree forever to be known as Camp Redeemer's Rest.

Being true to my Nam nature, I do not look back as I press forward in this lousy, good-for-nothing trench. Suddenly, I am in the middle of an internal battle to break free from my stubborn manner of self-survival by looking back for the very first time. The battle is intensified as I stop to stand still in my thoughts and prayers. Slowly, ever so slowly, I turn but stop midway, dropping my head in shame and turning to resume my walk forward.

From behind me, I hear Mike's voice as he says, "God bless you, Sojourner Robert. I love you as a brother."

I stop to stand still in my thoughts, fears, and prayers.

My internal battle rages on as I slowly, ever so slowly, turn around. Once again, at the midway point, I stop. This time, however, I pray for strength, courage, and freedom to do what I should have been doing all along: turning around to face friends and loved ones rather than running from them.

Closing my eyes and breathing deeply, I fight as never before to break free from this shackle of fear that has enslaved me from my Vietnam days. With God's help and Mike's encouraging words and my persistence, I finally turn to face a friend who has become a loved one in my family of faith, within my family of veterans, within my family known as Scholten. Our eyes meet through the grayish colors of the trench, our smiles meet in heaven, and our greetings of farewell are heard throughout the trench.

"Wow. I should do this more often," I say, turning to press forward once again.

"Yes, you should," I hear behind me.

Without effort, I turn around, responding to Mike with, "Yes, I shall. And I will do so in the name of my Redeemer, who is my Rest,[146] Comfort,[147] Joy,[148] and Strength."[149]

In turning to face my onward journey in the trench of PTSD sunken in the bottom of the valley of the shadow of death, the Lord speaks to my heart in how to press forward. I am to do so with Psalm 23 as a guide for my family who travels with me in PTSD.

EPILOGUE

Here in the Appalachian Hills of Jackson County, Kentucky, there is a simple farewell greeting folks share with one another: "Be safe."

Be safe, my friend.

It is my hope and prayer that 2 Timothy 4:18 holds true for you: "The Lord will rescue me from every evil deed and bring me safely into His heavenly kingdom. To Him be the glory forever and ever. Amen."

God bless you and encourage you in the reality of his amazing grace and unending mercy as you walk in his ways and on the paths he sets out before you.

Your fellow sojourner and friend, Pastor Bob "Preacher."

APPENDIX A: CONCLUDING PRAYER

Let me have the privilege to pray with you personally and for anybody else who has taken the journey thus far through the trench of PTSD.

"To You, oh Lord, I lift up my soul."

To you, oh Lord, my fellow vet and I lift up our souls, entrusting them to you. Encourage, we pray, our fellow veterans to do the same, for you are trustworthy, holy, and just.

"Oh, my God, I trust in You; let me not be ashamed; let not my enemies triumph over me."

Our God, we trust in you, as do many of our fellow veterans. We have tasted war with all is terribleness it dishes out to veterans and civilians alike. We despise the flavor it has left in our lives, yet many of our fellow veterans stand ready to go through it all again. We have learned the value of life and how fragile it truly is. We have learned the importance of faith and how strong it truly is. Father, keep our nation and those defending it safe. Do not let their enemies triumph over them nor over us. Let not our personal enemies of fear, anger, hatred, distrust, and lust triumph over us.

"Indeed, let no one who waits on You be ashamed; let those be ashamed who deal treacherously without cause."

Help us who are or have been caught up in the insanity of war to conduct our lives in such a way as not to be put to shame; nor to put our nation to shame; and, above all, put your name to shame.

"Show me Your ways, oh Lord; teach me Your paths."

Show me and my friend your ways so we do not go astray. Lead us daily all the days of our lives to you through your Spirit into the way and the truth and the life of your lordship over us.

"Lead me in Your truth and teach me, for You are the God of my salvation; on You do I wait all the day."

Teach both of us your paths, and assist us in our knowledge of your Word that is a map of righteousness to guide us through the mazes of life. Then encourage us to encourage each other and all those around us to do the same.

Help us who are yours to wait on you all day every day. Help us to do so in the knowledge of who you are and who we are in you. Please be with our fellow veterans who are not yet in a living relationship with you through your Son, Jesus Christ. Keep them safe, and draw them to yourself. We pray this on behalf of their families and ours too.

"Remember, oh Lord, Your tender mercies and Your lovingkindnesses, for they are from of old."

Remember, God, your tender mercies and your loving kindnesses, for they are of old, extending still to us here in the twenty-first century through your Son, our Savior. Thank you for the Beatitudes, of which, "Blessed are the merciful, for they shall obtain mercy," is one. Help us so to live, for we are always in need of mercy, especially me.

"Do not remember the sins of my youth, nor my transgressions; according to Your mercy remember me, for Your goodness' sake, oh Lord."

Oh, Lord, I confess before you, as did the Apostle Paul, that I am a sinner, a chief one at that. Therefore, I pray as did King David: "Do not remember the sins of my youth, nor my transgressions; according to your mercy remember me, for your goodness' sake, oh Lord."

As you have so wonderfully forgiven us who have come to you through your Son, help us forgive ourselves. And set us free from ourselves so we can live freely in our new natures in Christ Jesus. You no longer see our sins when we confess them to you with sincere hearts. Help us understand the significance of this glorious gift from your throne.

"Good and upright is the Lord; therefore He teaches sinners in the way."

Truly you are good and upright in all your ways, and all your ways are upright and good. Teach us your ways so we can live good and upright lives. We have seen so much that is not good and experienced that which is down-right wrong and evil. We desire to be good and upright but grow tired quickly from our prolonged battles with PTSD. We grow tired of being tired. Please refresh us in your goodness and teach us to number our days, knowing that each one is a gift from you.

I thank You, Lord, for this day in which life fills my soul and *new life* makes me whole. You have redeemed me and made me clean, setting me free to enjoy and serve you, my Redeemer. I once was lost, but you found me. I once was sinfully filthy and altogether ugly within, but you cleansed me and made me altogether lovely in your sight. I am humbly yours to deal with as you please.

"The humble He guides in justice, and the humble He teaches His way."

Help us and all our fellow veterans and all our families to have open and teachable hearts. Then lead us in your truth and teach us to apply it to all we do, say, and think. Lord Jesus Christ, help us to run to you and not from you, for you are the truth. Set us free in your Word to live your Word in this world, a true freedom only found in salvation through the blood and in the name of Jesus Christ, your Son.

"All the paths of the Lord are mercy and truth, to such as keep His covenant and His testimonies."

All your paths are mercy and truth to me and all others who keep your promise and testimonies. Lord, there are times when your path of mercy seems to have been stomped unmercifully into shattered pieces of crumbled hopes and dreams. I know this is not true. But down here in this miserable trench of PTSD, it seems all too real.

Oh Lord God Almighty, author of all life and truth, keep me ever so close to your Son, who is the Living Truth.

"For Your name's sake, oh Lord, pardon my iniquity, for it is great."

Take it from me, and remember it no more. For such love and mercy I worship you in truth and spirit, as do many of my fellow veterans. Help us who believe in Christ Jesus stay on the path you have chosen for us. Help us, oh Lord, to yearn to learn firsthand from your guiding hand.

"Who is the man who fears the Lord? Him shall He teach in the way He chooses."

Father, early in life, within my family and church, I was taught, nurtured, and encouraged in your Word. In those earlier years I did not appreciate the upmost importance of honoring your name, worshiping you, and obeying your Word. But I sure do now. Please continue teaching me to pray and live as I ought to in these troubled times.

> Our father which art in heaven, hallowed be thy name. Thy kingdom come. Thy will be done in earth as it is in heaven. Give us this day our daily bread. And forgive us our debts as we forgive our debtors. And lead us not into temptation, but deliver us from evil: for thine is the kingdom, and the power, and the glory, for ever. Amen.
>
> Matthew 6:9–13 (KJV)

He has shown you, oh man, what is good; and what does the Lord require of you but to do justly, to love mercy, and to walk humbly with your God?[150]

Help me so to live. Help me so to live, I pray. I ask this also on behalf of my fellow sojourners through this trench in the bottom of the valley of the shadow of death. Amen.

"He himself shall dwell in prosperity, and his descendents shall inherit the earth."

Oh Lord our Lord, help us be content with what we have this side of heaven, for all good gifts are from above. Bless our families with deep desires for being good stewards of creation and gentle servants of your kingdom within this world.

"The secret of the Lord is with those who fear Him, and He will show them His covenant."

Create a growing desire to carry your Word in our hearts, along with an ever-present willingness to share the hope that dwells within us.[151] Press upon our minds the reality of Jeremiah 33:3: "Call to Me, and I will answer you, and show you great and mighty things, which you do not know." Continue establishing a solid foundation of faith in our lives, for I, along with my fellow Christians, acknowledge the reality of Hebrews 12:1–2, that Jesus is the author and finisher of our faith and he daily blesses us with the blessing you taught Moses to teach Aaron and his sons to bless the people of God.

> The Lord bless you and keep you;
>
> The Lord make his face shine upon you,
>
> And be gracious to you;
>
> The Lord lift up His countenance upon you,
>
> And give you peace.[152]
>
> Numbers 6:24–26

"My eyes are ever toward the Lord, for He shall pluck my feet out of the net."

It pains me to confess there are times I take my eyes off you and your Word. In temporary blindness, I wander off and away from your path of truth, condemning me to a lifestyle of doing what is right in my own eyes, regardless of who I hurt or what comes about by my actions. Thank you, Lord, for having mercy on me by drawing me back to your pathway of truth. I pray all this also on behalf of my fellow veterans.

"Turn Yourself to me, and have mercy upon me, for I am desolate and afflicted."

Have mercy on us and especially on our families, for we have put them through so much. We also tenderly pray this for our fellow vets who have left trails of multiple broken families in this hideous trench of PTSD. Help us not to stand in judgment, but come alongside each and every person within these shattered marriages and families that PTSD broke into and scattered. God, my God, I humbly ask you to clear the way for your handpicked servants of reconciliation to each person's life, including my own.

"The troubles of my heart have enlarged; bring me out of my distress!"

Lord, trouble seems to be my middle name at times. I do not go looking for it, but it comes looking for me. Worries, concerns, and fears get the best of me at times. But I know better. I really do! This too I battle at times, resulting in added physical and emotional pressures to my heart.

Oh Lord, please give me eyes to see and ears to hear the troubles festering in my heart, especially those from my tour of duty in Vietnam. Some are slowly surfacing after all these decades, frustrating me. Your Word instructs me to cast all my cares and worries upon you because you care for me.[153] This I know and believe, yet I struggle at times. So I plead with thee, bring me out of my distress. This I pray also on behalf of my fellow veterans and their families and friends.

"Look upon my affliction and my pain, and forgive all my sins."

Affliction and pain have been my unwelcome traveling companions while traversing through this trench I have come to despise. I might despise this place, but you advise me within it. Forgive me for all the times I reject your advice, for each rejection has added fuel to the internal flames of affliction and pain. Look upon me, Lord, for it comforts me knowing I am not out of your sight.[154]

"Consider my enemies, for they are many; and they hate me with cruel hatred."

Lord, I no longer fight against humans with military weaponry, but I do fight in age-old battles between good and evil, truth and falsehood, righteousness and unrighteousness. You are my high rock from which I can see my enemy. You are my armor in which I can confidently stand up to them and courageously withstand their attacks. Please therefore consider my enemies, for they are far more than I can handle. Help me repel the arrows of hate, prejudice, anger, slanderous lies, and half-truths, threats and intimidations, along with untold others. Please help me and my fellow veterans fight evil with goodness, resisting all temptations to fight evil with evil.[155]

"Oh keep my soul, and deliver me; let me not be ashamed, for I put my trust in You."

Lord, there are times I feel surrounded by troubles not of my own making and circumstances beyond my control. During such times, please keep my soul and deliver me from me, lest I act inappropriately, bringing shame upon myself and your name. Help me trust you with all my heart. Help me resist leaning on my own understanding. And help me acknowledge you in all my ways.[156]

"Let integrity and uprightness preserve me, for I trust in You."

Help me to rejoice in hope, be patient in tribulation, and be steadfast in prayer.[157] Help me faithfully apply myself to Psalm 37:3–6:

> Trust in the Lord, and do good; dwell in the land,
> and feed on His righteousness. Delight yourself

also in the Lord, and He will give you the desires of your heart. Commit your way to the Lord, trust also in Him, and He shall bring it to pass. He shall bring forth your righteousness as the light, and your justice as the noonday.

"Redeem Israel, oh God, out of all their troubles."

Redeem me and my fellow veterans, oh Lord, out of all our troubles, which are many. Help us to trust you in all we do, for you are trustworthy in all your ways. Forgive us for the troubles we bring upon ourselves, and help us to forgive those who bring troubles upon us. And we thank you for the greatest redemption of all: our Lord, Jesus Christ, the Prince of peace, in whom alone there is salvation and enduring peace.

Dear heavenly Father, I bring this entire prayer to you on behalf of all who have traveled through this journey of *Psalm 25 and PTSD*. Please also encourage us to encourage each other and our loved ones and friends to pray through and accept the blessings of Psalm 103:

> Bless the Lord, O my soul; And all that is within me, bless His holy name! Bless the Lord, O my soul, And forget not all His benefits: Who forgives all your iniquities, Who heals all your diseases, Who redeems your life from destruction, Who crowns you with lovingkindness and tender mercies, Who satisfies your mouth with good things, So that your youth is renewed like the eagle's.

> The Lord executes righteousness And justice for all who are oppressed. He made known His ways to Moses, His acts to the children of Israel. The Lord is merciful and gracious, Slow to anger, and abounding in mercy. He will not always strive

with us, Nor will He keep His anger forever. He has not dealt with us according to our sins, Nor punished us according to our iniquities.

For as the heavens are high above the earth, So great is His mercy toward those who fear Him; As far as the east is from the west, So far has He removed our transgressions from us. As a father pities his children, So the Lord pities those who fear Him. For He knows our frame; He remembers that we are dust.

As for man, his days are like grass; As a flower of the field, so he flourishes. For the wind passes over it, and it is gone, And its place remembers it no more. But the mercy of the Lord is from everlasting to everlasting On those who fear Him, And His righteousness to children's children, To such as keep His covenant, And to those who remember His commandments to do them.

The Lord has established His throne in heaven, And His kingdom rules over all.

Bless the Lord, you His angels, Who excel in strength, who do His word, Heeding the voice of His word. Bless the Lord, all you His hosts, You ministers of His, who do His pleasure. Bless the Lord, all His works, In all places of His dominion. Bless the Lord, O my soul!

Psalm 103

APPENDIX B: COMING TO AN UNDERSTANDING

Cheryl and I were on a six-hour drive during which Cheryl was proofreading my manuscript. She does this proofreading out loud since I need to hear my words as well as read them. When she came to verse/chapter four, I saw her looking at me with a gaze I had never seen before. It was as if she had held back a troubling question for all too long.

In my soul, I knew what was begging to be asked, a question I'd preferably answer later not sooner. I knew what had to do be done.

"Honey, what's on your mind?"

"Bob, I just don't understand all this. I cannot see why you even think that way about yourself. That war is long over for you. You no longer have to fight it."

"No, it's not, Cheryl. It's not over for me at all."

"No, Bob. You no longer have to feel like you have to fight Vietnam all over again. Do you really feel trapped? Are you really that numb?"

"Cheryl, my love, it has nothing to do with you at all. It is this PTSD that I'm battling. And I'll be fighting it the rest of my life."

"But, Bob, you are a Christian, a strong one at that. And you are a pastor, a good one at that too."

"Honey, you are a devout Christian and mature in your faith. You are also well versed in the doctrines of the Bible. Are you not?"

"Yes. I guess I am."

"Cheryl, I know you are. You are a Christian with assurance of salvation strongly embedded in your soul. Now, upon the salvation of your soul, did God get rid of your old nature, or did it remain in you?"

"No. God did not get rid of it. And yes, I do have problems with my old nature. I have problems with it every day."

"Now think about this, Cheryl. Does that make you any less Christian?"

"No. Of course it doesn't."

"Cheryl, just like you have two natures that are at constant odds within you, so it is within me with PTSD. I'll fight this stuff and wrestle with it for the rest of my life. I would prefer not to. But that is impossible because PTSD is a natural reaction and byproduct of experiences in war. For me, it was Vietnam."

Watching my precious wife's eyes light up, I knew she finally got a small glimpse of understanding into the darkened trench of PTSD.

Turning to the Bible, we find examples of this old/ new nature at work in the Apostle Paul's life and ministry. If he, of all people, had difficulties with this old/new nature/life/man factor, who are we to think we will not be bothered by it?

In Paul's letter to the Christians in Rome around AD 56, Romans 7:14–25, he revealed his shortcomings for all to read, including us here in the twenty-first century. Why do such a thing? Simply put, to prepare his readers for lifelong internal battles between flesh and spirit and old and new natures. What a wonderful thought and gift.

Like it or not, accept it or not, deny it or not, we who have been set free through Jesus Christ must continue to flee from sin. The advice God gave Cain in Genesis 4:6–7 still holds true today: "Why are you angry? And why has your countenance fallen? If you do well, will you not be accepted? And if you do not well, sin lies at your door. And its desire is for you, but you should rule over it."

Then in Paul's letter to the Christians in Ephesus around AD 61, Ephesians 4:17–32, he gives much-needed practical advice pertaining to daily Christian living in their relationships with other people. In reading, reflecting on, and striving to apply Paul's advice, a comical thought comes to mind. It would be a whole lot easier to live a solid Christian life if there was nobody around to bother me.

The Apostle Paul continues advising, preparing, and encouraging his fellow Christians in the city of Colossae, Colossians 3:1–25, to live renewed lives in Christ through applying God's Word. Paul knew such living would bring forth peace in all their relationships, especially their families. He must have worn out his quill writing this much-needed letter to the first-century Colossian Christians and to us twenty-first-century believers.

I am no Apostle Paul, but I am one who has been challenged, influenced, and encouraged by his epistles in the living Word of God that always accomplish what God intends it to, as confirmed in Isaiah 55:10–11:

For as the rain comes down, and the snow from heaven, And do not return there, But water the earth, And make it bring forth and bud, That it may give seed to the sower And bread to the eater, So shall My word be that goes forth from My mouth; It shall not return to Me void, But it shall prosper in the thing for which I sent it.

SCRIPTURAL REFERENCES AND END NOTES

Introduction

1   Department of Veterans Affairs PTSD Residential Rehabilitation Program (Lexington, KY. Medical Center)

2   Ibid.; "PTSD And The Importance Of Finding Meaning," prepared by Cynthia E. Dunn, Ph.D., Licensed Psychologist, Clinical Coordinator, PTSD Clinical Team; 2 Timothy 2:4

3   Lawrence G. Calhoun and Richard G. Tedeschi, Editors. " Handbook of Post-traumatic Growth: Research and Practices;" Edited by. Lawrence Erlbaum Associates Inc, Publishers, 2006

4   Ibed.;

5   Robert G. Scholten. "Reflections on a Journey to War: Finding Hope Despite Yesterday's Shadow." Dumont, Iowa: Green Olive Tree Publishing Outreach, 2005. p. 73.

6   1 Corinthians 13:12–13

Lifting Up My Soul

Trust Is an Issue

Waiting Is Hard to Do

To Learn or Not to Learn

28 Psalm 119:105
29 2 Samuel 22:31
30 Ecclesiastics 12:1
31 Psalm 1:1–6, Psalm 119:33–40, James 1:5–8
32 Psalm 119:11, Psalm 139:23–24, Proverbs3:1–8, Romans 8:26–28
33 Hebrews 4:14–16, Hebrews 12:1–2
34 Psalm 19:7–11, Psalm 111:7–8, 2 Timothy 3:16–17, James 1:22–25

Running to or from the Truth

35 Psalm 5:8, Psalm 27:11–14, Psalm 27:1–5, Psalm 37:7

Mercy. Do I Deserve It?

36 Psalm 23:3, Psalm 51:10–12, Proverbs 13:1–2, Hebrews 6:11–12
37 Genesis 22:1–9, Exodus 3:1–6
38 Hebrews 13:8
39 1 Corinthians 1:9, 1 Thessalonians 5:23–24
40 Hebrews 10:22, Psalm 51:17
41 Hebrews 10:31, Isaiah 40:15
42 Psalm 8
43 John 16:7–15; 14:15–17, 25–27
44 Isaiah 55:10–11

Forgiveness. How Can I Be?

45 Matthew 11:28–30
46 Psalm 19:7–14, Romans 12:1–2, James 1:19–25
47 Hebrews 12:1–2
48 John 6:37–40
49 Hebrews 4:14–16

50   Psalm 95:6–7, Psalm 56:3–4, Jeremiah 17:7–8
51   Revelation 3:20

For Goodness's Sake. Knock! Knock!

52   2 Timothy 3:16–17, Jeremiah 17:7–8
53   "Jesus Loves Me," written by American author Anna Bartlett Warner (1827–1915)

Humble Justice versus Injustices

54   Psalm 23:6; 27:1–8, 13–14; 41:11–12; 63:6–8
55   Luke 16:19–31
56   John 14:27, 16:33; Romans 5:1–11; Philippians 4:4–7, cf. 6–7; 2 Thessalonians 3:16
57   Galatians 6:7–10, James 1:12–15
58   Psalm 37:23–24 and 28, Isaiah 30:18

Choosing Wisely. Learning to Choose

59   Philippians 4:6–7
60   Job 4:5–6, Hebrews 3:5–6, James 4:10
61   Matthew 6:30–34; Matthew 14:28–32, cf. 31; Mark 11:20–25
62   Matthew 14:28–29
63   Psalm 139:1–12, Matthew 28:18–20
64   James 1:16–18, John 3:27
65   Mark 9:17–29
66   Zechariah 4:6

Pardon My Iniquity Please

67   2 Corinthians 10:3–4
68   Romans 8:31–39, Hebrews 4:13, Psalm 121, Deuteronomy 31:6–8
69   Exodus 20:7

70   Galatians 4:1–7
71   Romans 5:10–11
72   2 Corinthians 5:18–19
73   Colossians 3:12–17
74   Leviticus 19:17–18, John 13:34–35
75   Judges 6:36–40
76   Exodus 3:9–4:17
77   Exodus 16:1–22
78   Judges 16:1–21
79   2 Samuel 11:1–12:14
80   Genesis 16:1–6
81   Luke 19:1–10
82   Luke 10:38–42
83   Luke 22:31–34
84   Romans 8:26–28

Holy Fear versus Oh Dear

85   Psalm 27:1, Romans 13:11–14
86   Ephesians 3:14–21, 1 Peter 1:3–9
87   Psalm 139:23–24, Romans 8:26–27
88   Jeremiah 7:9–10, 29:11–13; Matthew 6:19–21,
      22:37–40
89   Exodus 34:6–9, Psalm 100:1–5, John 15:9–17,
      Romans 5:6–11
90   John 10:27–30
91   Ephesians 1:1–14, 1 Peter 1:3–7
92   Psalm 73:25–26
93   John 6:37–40, 10:28–30

Hope for Those Brutalized by PTSD

94   Psalm 51:9–12
95   Romans 15:1–7, 2 Corinthians 1:3–5

96   1 Timothy 6:13–15
97   John 1:1–5, 2 Timothy 3:16–17
98   John 3:16
99   John 1:14, Romans 5:1–5
100 2 Timothy 1:8–10
101 Acts 2:20

A Secret Well Worth Knowing

102 Hebrews 4:12–13, Revelations 2:12–17
103 Psalm 19:7–11, Isaiah 55:10–11, Hebrew 4:12–13
104 Psalm 91:1–4, Isaiah 41:10
105 Psalm 32:8–9, Psalm 73:23–26
106 Romans 12:1–2, Philippians 2:12–16, 1 John 5:13–15

Loneliness: An Ever-present Battle

107 James 2:13

Troubled Heart: Coming Up Out of Distress

108 Romans 12:1–2, Ephesians 6:14–15
109 John Calvin. "Commentary on the Book of Psalms." Vol. 1. Grand Rapids Michigan: Baker Book House Company, Reprinted 1984. p. *432*; Psalm 25:16–18

Affliction and Pain: Surviving PTSD's Dual Life

110 Psalm 37:7–8, Isaiah 40:31, James 5:7–11
111 Ephesians 3:14–21
112 Proverbs 31:10–31

Enemies Among Us: But There Is a Table

1131 Peter 3:12

114 John 10:1–5, Hebrews 3:7–15, Revelations 3:20

115 Jeremiah 17:9–10

116 John 8:12, 2 Samuel 22:29–31, Psalm 119:105, Proverbs 6:23

117 Matthew 26:1–27:66, John 19:17–42, 1 Corinthians 6:11, Colossians 1:19–23

118 Matthew 28:1–10, Mark 16:1–11, John 20:1–10

119 Matthew 28:1–10, Luke 24:50–53

120 Acts 2:1–47, Romans 8:12–17, 2 Corinthians 1:20–22, Ephesians 1:13–14 and 4:30

121 Ephesians 1:3–10 and 2:8–10

122 John 5:30, John 6:37–40

123 Galatians 4:4–7

124 John 1:29, Romans 5:6–11, Colossians 1:19–20, 1 John 1:7, Revelations 1:4–8 and 5:11–12

125 Matthew 22:11–14, cf. verse 14

126 John 15:16–17

127 1 Peter 1:17–19, cf. verse 19; John 1:29

Integrity: Learning the Truth About Truth

128 1 Peter 4:12–19

129 John 14:6, Hebrews 13:8, John 8:31–38, Psalm 119:151–152, Proverbs 30:5–6

130 Exodus 20:1–17

131 Psalm 19:7–11, Psalm 119:159–160, Proverbs 30:5, 2 Timothy 2:15 and 3:14–17

132 Psalm 37:3–4

133 Matthew 11:28–30; Psalm 116:1–19, cf. verse 7; Jeremiah 6:16

134 Matthew 28:20, John 14:15–18

Camp Redeemer's Rest

135 1 Peter 1:22–25
136 1 Corinthians 13:13, Galatians 6:9–10, Ephesians 1:15, 2 Timothy 2:22
137 Isaiah 29:16 and 64:8, Jeremiah 18:1–6, Romans 9:20–21
138 John 15:1–11
139 Romans 15:1–7, Colossians 1:1–3
140 Psalm 103; Romans 3:3, 3:21–26, 8:18–30
141 Psalm 91:1–6, Isaiah 25:4
142 Romans 8:31–39
143 Psalm 91:1–6
144 Psalm 23:1–3, Psalm 42:1–11, Isaiah 53:4–6, Lamentations 3:19–26, Malachi 4:2
145 Psalm 14, Isaiah 53:4–12, John 8:32, 1 Peter 2:24–25
146 Matthew 11:28–30
147 Isaiah 51:12–13
148 John 15:11
149 Exodus 15:1–19, Psalm 28:6–9, Isaiah 40:28–31

Appendix A: Concluding Prayer

150 Micah 6:8
151 1 Peter 3:13–16
152 Numbers 6:24–26
153 1 Peter 5:6–7
154 Psalm 33:18–22
155 Romans 12:9–21
156 Proverbs 3:5–6
157 Romans 12:12